THE TOP
AIR FRYER
Recipe Book with Pictures

Super-Easy & Delicious Air Fryer Recipes and 4 Weeks Meal Plan
for Anyone to Cooking Air Fryer Food

Phoebe Charlton

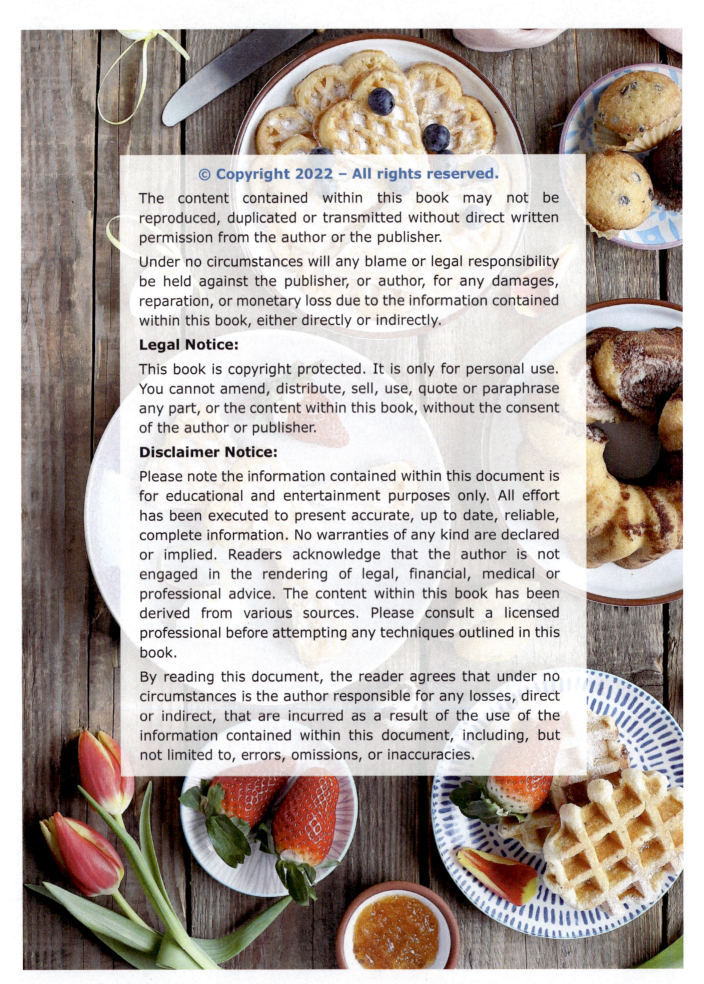

© Copyright 2022 – All rights reserved.

The content contained within this book may not be reproduced, duplicated or transmitted without direct written permission from the author or the publisher.

Under no circumstances will any blame or legal responsibility be held against the publisher, or author, for any damages, reparation, or monetary loss due to the information contained within this book, either directly or indirectly.

Legal Notice:

This book is copyright protected. It is only for personal use. You cannot amend, distribute, sell, use, quote or paraphrase any part, or the content within this book, without the consent of the author or publisher.

Disclaimer Notice:

Please note the information contained within this document is for educational and entertainment purposes only. All effort has been executed to present accurate, up to date, reliable, complete information. No warranties of any kind are declared or implied. Readers acknowledge that the author is not engaged in the rendering of legal, financial, medical or professional advice. The content within this book has been derived from various sources. Please consult a licensed professional before attempting any techniques outlined in this book.

By reading this document, the reader agrees that under no circumstances is the author responsible for any losses, direct or indirect, that are incurred as a result of the use of the information contained within this document, including, but not limited to, errors, omissions, or inaccuracies.

Table of Contents

Introduction 5

The Fundamentals of an Air Fryer 6

What Is an Air Fryer? 6
The General Benefits of an Air Fryer 6
The Health Benefits of an Air Fryer.......... 7
Step-By-Step Air Frying...................... 8
Arrange Your Food in the Air Fryer 9
Cooking Time and Temperature for Various Recipes 10
Straight from the Shop...................... 15
Cleaning Your Air Fryer..................... 15
Caring for Your Air Fryer 16
FAQs... 16

4-Week Meal Plan.......................... 19

Week 1 19
Week 2 19
Week 3 20
Week 4 20

Chapter 1 Breakfast Recipes 21

Strawberry Almonds Porridge 21
Salmon in Honey-Miso Sauce................ 21
Ham Omelet with Vegetable 21
Red Potatoes & Peppers 22
Cheese Sausage Frittata 22
Fried Potato Pieces........................... 22
Buttermilk Biscuits........................... 23
Easy Egg Rolls................................ 23
Crumbled Sausage Pizza..................... 23
Butter Banana Bread......................... 24
Egg Toast Cups 24
Cauliflower Fritters 24
Potato Pancakes 25
Cheese Onion Stuffed Peppers 25
Spinach Pie with Cheese 25
Baked Cinnamon Rolls 26
Dijon Feta Shakshuka......................... 26
Egg Potato Burrito 27
Walnut Courgette Bread 27

Chapter 2 Snacks and Appetizers Recipes 28

Crispy Pumpkin Seeds 28
Easy French Fries 28
Breaded Courgette Sticks 28
Crispy Cheese Sticks 29
Crispy Potato Chips.......................... 29
Cheese Spinach Rolls 29
Grilled Corn 30
Crusted Chicken Tenders 30

Savory Chickpeas............................. 30
Avocado Fries................................ 31
Tasty Crackers 31
Wrapped Avocado 31
Crispy Sweet Potato Chips 32
Fried Ravioli 32
Exotic Chicken Meatballs 32
Mac & Cheese Balls 33

Chapter 3 Vegetables and Sides Recipes 34

Palatable Brussels Sprouts................... 34
Spicy Okra Fries.............................. 34
Herbed Cauliflower Florets................... 34
Green Beans and Mushrooms................. 35
Onion & Sweet Potato 35
Flavourful Parmesan Aubergine 35
Tofu Cubes 36
Spiced Pumpkin Pieces....................... 36
Cheese Broccoli Gratin 36
Tangy Cauliflower............................ 37
Golden Onion Rings.......................... 37
Parmesan Brussels Sprout 37
Cauliflower Tacos 38
Simple Cheese Balls 38
Mini Tofu Bites 39
Chickpeas Falafels with Tahini Sauce 39
Cauliflower Fritters with Parmesan.......... 40
Cheese Stuffed Mushrooms 40

Chapter 4 Fish and Seafood Recipes.....41

Breaded Cod Fillets 41
Chili Tilapia 41
Panko-Crusted Prawn......................... 41
Lemon-Flavored Salmon...................... 42
Flavourful Tilapia Fillets...................... 42
Rosemary Salmon 42
Red Snapper with Lemon Slices.............. 43
Fried Catfish Fillets........................... 43
Crisp Flounder Fillets 43
Grilled Lobster Tail 44
Garlicky Salmon.............................. 44
Jumbo Lump Crab Cakes 44
Cod Fillets.................................... 45
Tuna Cakes 45
Cheese Fillets 45
Tasty Salmon Fillets.......................... 46
Fish Pineapple Mix........................... 46
Mackerel Fillets.............................. 46
Seasoned Prawn 47
Polenta Squid 47

Fish Fingers 47
Tilapia Tacos with Sauce 48
Crab Meat Prawn Roll 48
Prawn Stuffed Peppers 49
Flounder Fillets............................ 49

Chapter 5 Chicken and Poultry Recipes 50

Baked Turkey Breast 50
Chicken Pot Pie 50
Whole Cooked Chicken 51
Crusted Chicken Thighs 51
Rustic Whole Chicken 51
Cream Chicken Parmigiana................... 52
Peanut Butter Chicken Thighs............... 52
Crunchy Chicken Strips....................... 52
Savory Chicken Breasts 53
Veggies & Chicken Breasts 53
Chicken Wings with Teriyaki Sauce 53
Spiced Chicken in Egg Mixture.............. 54
Chicken Thighs with Sesame Seeds 54
Hot Fried Chicken 55
Curry Chicken Wings 55
Herbed Turkey Roast 56
Herb Chicken Thighs 56
Homemade Popcorn Chicken 57
Veggies Chicken Pie 57
Marinated Turkey Thighs...................... 58
Turkey Breast and Bacon 58
Spiced Turkey Breast.......................... 59
Panko Chicken Wings 59

Chapter 6 Beef, Pork, and Lamb Recipes
.... 60

Steak with Chimichurri Sauce............... 60
Beef and Broccoli Florets 60
Honey-Glazed Pork Chops 61
Rosemary Lamb Roast......................... 61
Braised Steak................................... 61

Mini Beef Burger 62
Lemon Lamb Chops............................ 62
Roasted Skirt Steaks 62
Pork Chops..................................... 63
Rib-eye Steak.................................. 63
Mongolian Beef................................. 63
Simple-Seasoned Beef 64
Beef Kebabs 64
Roasted Steak 64
BBQ Pork Ribs 65
Pork Tenderloin with Peach Salsa........... 65
Butter Sirloin Steaks.......................... 65
Flavourful Leg of Lamb 66
Vegetables & Bacon Burgers 66
Short Beef Ribs................................ 67
Simple Lamb Chops............................ 67
Homemade Pork Tenderloin 68

Chapter 7 Desserts Recipes.................. 69

Cinnamon Bread Pudding 69
Blueberry Crumble 69
Homemade Smores 69
Cinnamon Apricot 70
Vanilla Pecan Brownies........................ 70
Butter Peanut Cookies 70
Apple Fritters 71
Pumpkin Muffins 71
Cinnamon Pear Halves 71
Tasty Chocolate Donuts....................... 72
Hazelnut Chocolate Brownies 72

Conclusion 73

Appendix 1 Measurement Conversion Chart 74

Appendix 2 Recipes Index.................. 75

Introduction

It's no secret that oil is not beneficial for our health, and studies have shown that consuming too much fat can lead to weight gain, heart disease, and cancer. For this reason, it's essential to carefully consider the amount of oil we use in our cooking. When possible, we should opt for recipes that call for a minimum amount of oil. Doing so will not only help to reduce our overall intake of fat but also help to improve the taste and texture of our food. In addition, minimal-oil recipes often require less time and effort to prepare, making them a convenient option for busy weeknights.

Regarding healthier cooking methods, air fryers are the clear winner. Air fryers utilize little to no oil, resulting in food that contains up to 80% less fat than its fried counterparts. In addition, air fryers cook food evenly and quickly, meaning fewer nutrients are lost in the cooking process. And since air fryers circulate hot air around the food, there's no risk of the formation of harmful compounds like acrylamide. An air fryer is the best option for making healthy food if you want to reduce calories or exposure to harmful chemicals.

Air fryers have recently gained much popularity for their ability to cook food quickly and with little to no oil. This cooking method has led to healthier versions of many popular fried foods, such as French fries, chicken wings, and mozzarella sticks. Air fryer food is healthier than its traditional counterparts and is also considered to be more flavourful and crispy. One reason is that air fryers use very little oil, allowing the food's natural flavours to shine through. Additionally, air fryers cook food at a higher temperature than deep fryers, which helps to create a crispier exterior. As a result, air fryer food is often considered superior in taste and healthiness.

The Fundamentals of an Air Fryer

What Is an Air Fryer?

An Air Fryer is a versatile kitchen device that cooks food by circulating hot air around it. It uses a fan to circulate hot air around the food, which cooks it and gives it a crispy, fried texture. Air fryers are typically small and compact, making them easy to store on a countertop or in a cabinet. Most air fryers have a basket or tray that holds the food and a timer that lets you set how long the food should be cooked. Some air fryers also have temperature controls, so you can make sure the food is cooked at the right temperature. When using an air fryer, you can cook food with little to no oil, reducing fat and calories in your meal. Additionally, air fryers cook food quickly and evenly, so you can avoid overcooking or undercooking your food.

Unlike traditional frying methods, air fryers use little or no oil to cook food. This reduction in oil not only reduces the amount of fat in your food, but it can also help to reduce the formation of carcinogens. In addition, air fryers cook food more quickly than conventional methods, making them a convenient option for busy families. Air fryers are also extremely versatile, able to cook a wide variety of foods. Whether you're looking to make a healthy snack or a full meal, an air fryer can help you do so with ease. With so many advantages, it's no wonder air fryers are becoming a kitchen staple in homes across the country.

The General Benefits of an Air Fryer

Air fryers are all the rage nowadays, and it's little wonder why. These versatile little appliances can do everything from frying up a juicy steak to baking a delicious cake. Best of all, air fryers are much healthier than traditional fryers because they use little or no oil. Here are some benefits of using an air fryer:

- It cooks food evenly.
- You can cook various foods in it, including meat, vegetables, and even desserts.

- It's much healthier than other traditional frying methods because there's minimal use of oil.
- Air-fried food is crispy on the outside and tender on the inside.
- You can save money as you'll be buying much less oil.
- Air fryers are compact and take up less space than traditional deep fryers.
- Using one is safer than traditional deep fryers because there's no risk of oil splattering or fires.
- You have access to control the temperature and cooking time easily with an air fryer, so you'll never overcook or burn your food.
- Air-fried food doesn't have that greasy taste or feel that deep-fried food does.
- Many air fryers come with accessories that allow you to cook multiple types of food at once.
- Most air fryers have a removable basket that makes it easy to transfer food to a serving plate when it's done cooking.
- Air-fried food retains more nutrients than deep-fried food because it's cooked with less heat exposure.
- Cooking times for air-fried foods are shorter than their deep-fried counterparts.
- You won't need to ventilate your kitchen when using an air fryer because there's little or no smoke
- Cleanup is a breeze with an air fryer; simply remove the basket and wash it in soapy water.
- Many air fryers come with a recipe manual so you can start cooking immediately.
- Air frying is a versatile cooking method that can be used for both savoury and sweet dishes.
- Air-fried foods are suitable for those on a low-fat diet.
- An air fryer makes a great gift for anyone who loves to cook!

The Health Benefits of an Air Fryer

The air fryer is a popular kitchen appliance that cooks food by circulating hot air around it. The food is cooked in a basket or tray with little or no oil, making it a healthier option than deep-fried food. Here are some of the health benefits of using an air fryer:

- Helps reduce the amount of fat in your food.
- Helps reduce the number of calories in your food.
- Helps preserve the nutrients in your food.
- Helps reduce the risk of cancer and other diseases.
- Can be beneficial for digestion and metabolism.
- Can help to reduce cholesterol and triglyceride levels in your blood.
- Can help improve your heart health.
- Can be effective in regulating blood sugar levels.
- Helps to boost your immune system.
- Helps you to lose weight healthily.

Step-By-Step Air Frying

This cooking process may seem a bit daunting if you're new to air frying. But once you get the hang of it, you'll be churning out delicious, crispy meals in no time! Here's a step-by-step guide to air frying:

Prepare the Air Fryer Basket

Before you start cooking with your air fryer, it's important to grease the basket or pan with cooking spray. Doing so will help to prevent sticking and make cleanup a breeze. Simply spray the inside of the basket or pan with cooking spray and then slide your food inside. If you're unsure how much to use, start with a light coating and then add more as needed. Be sure to coat the entire surface, including the sides and bottom. Otherwise, you may find that your food sticks or burns. Once you've finished cooking, simply wipe out the basket or pan with a paper towel or dishcloth.

Adjust the Temperature

Most air fryers have a preheat function, so you can preheat the air fryer for 5 minutes before you start cooking. If you don't have a preheat function, you can set the temperature to the required setting and wait 5 minutes before you start cooking. It's important to note that different foods require different cooking times and temperatures. For instance, chicken wings will cook more quickly than chicken breasts. As a general rule of thumb, smaller pieces of food cook more quickly than larger pieces. Therefore, it's essential to keep an eye on the food as it cooks and to adjust the time and temperature accordingly. With a bit of practice, you'll be able to cook any type of food in your air fryer perfectly.

Preheat the Air Fryer

To preheat the air fryer, simply set it to the desired temperature and let it run for a few minutes before adding your food. Preheating the appliance will help to ensure that your food is cooked evenly and prevents it from sticking to the bottom of the basket. Additionally, preheating the air fryer will help to seal in flavours and prevent them from being lost during cooking.

Arrange Your Food in the Air Fryer

After preheating your air fryer, it's time to add your food. You'll want to begin by arranging your food in the basket, leaving space between each piece. Common items that are cooked in an air fryer include chicken, meat, and vegetables. In some recipes, you may also place baking pans with ingredients such as omelettes, quiches, cakes, bread, and muffins inside the basket. No matter what you're cooking, following these simple tips will help you get the best results.

Set the Required Time

To start cooking, slide the basket inside and set the required time. This may look like an easy task, but there are a few things to keep in mind. First, ensure that the basket is positioned correctly in the fryer; if it's not, the food may not cook evenly. Second, set the timer according to the recipe or cooking instructions. If you're not sure about the cooking time, stay on the side of caution and start with a shorter cooking time. You can always add more time according to your requirements.

Press Start

After placing the food inside the basket and setting the time, press the start button to begin cooking the food in the air fryer. The indicator light turns on to show that the air fryer is operational. Some models of air fryers also have a pause button that can be used to halt the cooking process if necessary.

Flip the Food

While using an air fryer, it's important to flip the food occasionally to ensure even cooking. This is important for thick portions/pieces of food or those with a lot of surface area, as they can cook unevenly if left in one position for too long. To ensure that your food cooks evenly, consult your recipe and flip the food accordingly. For example, if the recipe says to cook for 10 minutes and then flip, set a timer for 5 minutes and then flip the food over. By flipping the food regularly, you can help to ensure that it cooks evenly and comes out perfect every time.

After cooking time is completed, remove the food from the air fryer and serve accordingly. Make sure to use oven mitts or gloves, as the food will be hot. If you're not serving the food immediately, place it on a plate or cutting board to cool. Once it's cooled, you can cut it into smaller pieces or serve it as is.

Cooking Time and Temperature for Various Recipes

Air fryers are one of the hottest kitchen appliances on the market right now. And for good reason! They allow you to cook all of your favourite fried foods with little to no oil, making them healthier and less messy. But if you've never used an air fryer before, you may wonder what the best cooking times and temperatures are for different recipes. The fact is that it varies depending on what you're cooking. The examples below provide some different recipes and their corresponding cooking times in an air fryer.

As you can see, cooking times can vary depending on the recipe. It's important to experiment and find the cooking time that works best for your particular air fryer and your recipe. With a bit of practice, you'll be able to produce perfectly cooked meals in your air fryer in no time!

French Toast

- Grease the air fryer pan with cooking spray and then slide it inside the air fryer.
- Adjust the temperature of the air fryer to 200°C to preheat for 5 minutes.
- Press the "Start/Pause" button to start preheating.
- Add all the ingredients except bread slices and mix well in a large bowl.
- Coat the bread slices with your egg mixture evenly.
- After preheating, arrange the bread slices into the preheated air fryer pan.
- Slide the pan inside and set the time for 5 minutes.
- Press the "Start/Pause" button to start cooking.
- After 2½ minutes of cooking, press the "Start/Pause" button to pause cooking.
- Flip the slices and again press the "Start/Pause" button to resume cooking.
- After cooking time is finished, remove the French toast from the air fryer and serve warm.

Banana Bread

- Grease a loaf pan with cooking spray.
- In a stand mixer bowl, add all the ingredients and mix well.
- Place the mixture into the prepared loaf pan.

- Slide the air fryer basket inside the air fryer and adjust the temperature to 165°C to preheat for 5 minutes.
- Press the "Start/Pause" button to start preheating.
- After preheating, arrange the loaf pan into the air fryer basket.
- Slide the basket inside and set the time for 20 minutes.
- Press the "Start/Pause" button to start cooking.
- After cooking time is finished, remove the bread pan from the air fryer and place the pan onto a wire rack for about 10 to 15 minutes.
- Then invert the bread onto a wire rack to cool completely before slicing.
- Cut the bread into desired-sized slices and serve.

Chicken Thighs

- Add all the ingredients except for the lemon slices and toss to coat well in a large bowl.
- Refrigerate to marinate overnight.
- Remove the chicken thighs and let any excess marinade drip off.
- Grease the air fryer basket with cooking spray and then slide inside.
- Adjust the temperature of the air fryer to 180°C to preheat for 5 minutes.
- Press the "Start/Pause" button to start preheating.
- After preheating, arrange the chicken thighs into the air fryer basket.
- Slide the basket inside and set the time for 20 minutes.
- Press the "Start/Pause" button to start cooking.
- After 10 minutes of cooking, press the "Start/Pause" button to pause cooking.
- Flip the chicken thighs and again press the "Start/Pause" button to resume cooking.
- After cooking time is finished, remove the chicken thighs from the air fryer and serve hot alongside the lemon slices.

Turkey Breast

- Mix the herbs, brown sugar, and spices in a bowl.
- Coat the turkey breast evenly with oil and then generously rub it with the herb mixture.
- Adjust the temperature to 180°C to preheat for 5 minutes.
- Press the "Start/Pause" button to start preheating.
- After preheating, arrange the turkey breast into the air fryer basket, skin-side down.
- Slide the basket inside the air fryer and set the time for 35 minutes.
- Press the "Start/Pause" button to start cooking.
- After 18 minutes of cooking, press the "Start/Pause" button to pause cooking.
- Flip the turkey breast and again press the "Start/Pause" button to resume cooking.
- After cooking time is finished, remove the turkey breast from the air fryer and place it onto a cutting board for about 10 minutes before slicing.

Crumbed Sirloin Steak

- In a shallow bowl, place the flour.
- Crack the eggs in a second bowl and beat well.
- In a third bowl, mix together the panko and spices.
- Coat each steak with the flour, then dip into the beaten eggs and finally coat with the panko mixture.
- Grease the air fryer basket properly with cooking spray and then slide it inside the air fryer.
- Adjust the temperature of the air fryer to 180°C to preheat for 5 minutes.
- Press the "Start/Pause" button to start preheating.
- After preheating, arrange the steaks in the air fryer basket.
- Slide the basket inside the air fryer and set the time for 10 minutes.
- Press the "Start" button.
- After cooking time is finished, remove the steaks from the air fryer and serve immediately.

BBQ Pork Chops

- With a meat mallet, thoroughly pound the pork chops.
- Sprinkle the chops with a little salt and black pepper.
- Add the BBQ sauce and chops to a large bowl and mix well.
- Refrigerate, covered for about 6 to 8 hours.
- Remove the chops from the bowl and discard the excess sauce.
- Grease the air fryer basket with cooking spray and then slide it inside the air fryer.
- Adjust the temperature of the air fryer to 180°C to preheat for 5 minutes.
- Press the "Start/Pause" button to start preheating.
- After preheating, arrange the pork chops in the air fryer basket.
- Slide the basket inside the air fryer and set the time for 16 minutes.
- Press the "Start/Pause" button to start cooking.
- After 8 minutes of cooking, press the "Start/Pause" button to pause cooking.
- Flip the chops and again press the "Start/Pause" button to resume cooking.
- After cooking time is finished, remove the chops from the air fryer and serve hot.

Herbed Leg of Lamb

- Coat the leg of lamb with oil and sprinkle with salt and black pepper.
- Wrap the leg of lamb with the sprigs of herbs.
- Grease the air fryer basket with cooking spray and then slide it inside the air fryer.
- Adjust the temperature of the air fryer to 150°C to preheat for 5 minutes.
- Press the "Start/Pause" button to start preheating.
- After preheating, arrange the leg of lamb in the air fryer basket.
- Slide the basket inside the air fryer and set the time for 75 minutes.
- Press the "Start/Pause" button to start cooking.
- After 45 minutes of cooking, press the "Start/Pause" button to pause cooking.
- Flip the leg of lamb and again press the "Start/Pause" button to resume cooking.
- After cooking time is finished, remove the leg of lamb from the air fryer and place it onto a platter.
- Thoroughly cover the leg of lamb for about 10 minutes before slicing.
- Cut the leg of lamb into desired size pieces and serve.

Maple Salmon

- Sprinkle the salmon fillets evenly with salt and then coat them with maple syrup.
- Grease the air fryer basket with cooking spray and then slide it inside the air fryer.
- Adjust the temperature to 180°C to preheat for 5 minutes.
- Press the "Start/Pause" button to start preheating.
- After preheating, arrange the salmon fillets in the air fryer basket in a single layer.
- Slide the basket inside the air fryer and set the time for 8 minutes.
- Press the "Start/Pause" button to start cooking.
After cooking time is finished, remove the salmon fillets from the air fryer and serve hot

Shrimp Kebabs

- Mix the lemon juice, garlic, and spices in a bowl.
- Add the shrimp and mix well.
- Thread the shrimp onto pre-soaked wooden skewers.
- Grease the air fryer basket with cooking spray and then slide it inside the air fryer.
- Adjust the temperature to 175°C to preheat for 5 minutes.
- Press the "Start/Pause" button to start preheating.
- After preheating, arrange the shrimp skewers into the air fryer basket in a single layer.
- Slide the basket inside and set the time for 8 minutes.
- Press the "Start/Pause" button to start cooking.
- After 4 minutes of cooking, press the "Start/Pause" button to pause cooking.
- Flip the skewers and again press the "Start/Pause" button to resume cooking.
- After cooking time is finished, remove the shrimp skewers from the air fryer and serve.

Parmesan Brussels Sprouts

• Grease the air fryer basket with cooking spray and then slide it inside the air fryer.
• Adjust the temperature to 200°C to preheat for 5 minutes.
• Press the "Start/Pause" button to start preheating.
• Mix the Brussels sprouts, vinegar, oil, salt, and black pepper in a bowl.
• After preheating, arrange the Brussels sprouts into the air fryer basket in a single layer.
• Slide the basket inside the air fryer and set the time for 10 minutes.
• Press the "Start/Pause" button.
• After 5 minutes of cooking, press the "Start/Pause" button.
• Flip the Brussels sprouts and sprinkle them with the breadcrumbs, followed by the cheese.
• Again, press the "Start/Pause" button to resume cooking.
• After cooking time is finished, remove the Brussels sprouts from the air fryer and serve hot.

Ratatouille

• Grease a baking pan with cooking spray.
• Add the vegetables, garlic, Herbs de Provence, oil, vinegar, salt, and black pepper in a large bowl and toss to coat well.
• Place the vegetable mixture into the prepared baking pan.
• Slide the air fryer basket inside and adjust the temperature to 180°C to preheat for 5 minutes.
• Press the "Start/Pause" button to start preheating.
• After preheating, arrange the baking pan into the air fryer basket.
• Slide the basket inside the air fryer and set the time for 15 minutes.
• Press the "Start/Pause" button to start cooking.
• After cooking time is finished, remove the baking pan from the air fryer and serve hot.

Roasted Cashews

• In a bowl, mix all the ingredients.
• Grease the air fryer basket with cooking spray and then slide it inside the air fryer.
• Adjust the temperature of the air fryer to 180°C to preheat for 5 minutes.
• Press the "Start/Pause" button to start preheating.
• After preheating, arrange the cashews into the air fryer basket in a single layer.
• Slide the basket inside the air fryer and set the time for 5 minutes.
• Serve hot or cooled.

Straight from the Shop

Opening an air fryer for the first time can be a little daunting, but following these simple tips will help to ensure that the process goes smoothly:

- Make sure that the air fryer is placed on a level surface.
- Remove all of the accessories from the interior of the appliance.
- Brush any loose debris from the heating element and oil pan.
- Wash the accessories and wipe the interior and exterior of the air fryer with a damp cloth. Ensure everything is dry before use.

Once the air fryer is clean, it's time to add oil. Use high-quality cooking oil and only fill the pan to the "max" line. Finally, plug in the air fryer and allow it to preheat for 3 to 5 minutes before adding food. By following these steps, you'll be well on your way to becoming an air fryer pro in no time!

Cleaning Your Air Fryer

An air fryer is a fantastic kitchen gadget that can be used to cook a variety of foods. While it's easy to use, it's important to clean the air fryer regularly to prevent the build-up of grease and food particles. Here are five steps for cleaning an air fryer:

- Unplug the air fryer and allow it to cool completely.
- Remove the basket and pan from the air fryer. Wash the pan and basket in warm, soapy water. If there is any hardened grease or food residue, scrub with a non-abrasive sponge or brush.
- With the help of a soft cloth or brush, wipe down the inside of the air fryer unit, being careful not to touch the heating element.
- Wipe down the outside of the unit with a damp cloth.
- Once everything is clean, dry all parts thoroughly before reassembling the air fryer and plugging it back in.

Caring for Your Air Fryer

An air fryer is an alternative to deep frying food in oil, and it can be used to cook a variety of food items in a healthy way. If you have an air fryer, here are five tips for taking care of it:

• Read the Manual: Before using your air fryer for the first time, be sure to read the manual. This will ensure that you understand how to operate the appliance and how to keep it clean.

• Preheat the Air Fryer: Most air fryers require preheating before cooking. This step is vital because it helps to ensure that your food cooks evenly.

• Don't Overcrowd the Basket: When cooking in an air fryer, it's important not to put too much in the basket, as this will stop the hot air from circulating properly and could result in uneven cooking.

• Shake the Basket: If you're cooking food like French fries or chicken tenders, be sure to shake the basket occasionally during cooking. This will help to ensure that all sides of the food are exposed to the hot air and therefore cook evenly.

• Allow the Air Fryer to Cool Down: After cooking, be sure to allow your air fryer to cool down before cleaning it. This can help prevent any appliance damage and make cleanup easier.

FAQs

How does an air fryer work?

Air fryers work by circulating hot air around the food, cooking the food quickly and evenly. Air fryers typically have a basket or tray that holds the food and a heating element that heats the air.

How do I choose the best air fryer for me?

When choosing an air fryer, there are several things you should keep in mind. First, consider how often you will use it and what you will be cooking with it. If you plan to use it frequently, you may want to invest in a higher-quality model. Second, think about capacity; how much food do you want to be able to cook at one time? Finally, consider your budget, as air fryers have a wide range of prices.

How do I use an air fryer?

Most air fryers come with detailed instructions on how to use them safely and effectively. In general, you'll preheat the machine, then add your food to the basket or tray. Make sure not to overcrowd the basket, as this can result in uneven cooking. Cook according to your recipe or desired doneness; most air fryers have timers and temperature controls to help with this process. When finished cooking, remove the basket or tray from the machine and allow the food to cool before eating.

Can I put aluminium foil in an air fryer?

Yes, you can use aluminium foil; however, there are a few things you need to remember if doing so. You should never line the bottom of the pan with foil, as this could start a fire. Also, ensure not to touch the heating element with foil, as this could cause a short circuit. We recommend spraying a little cooking spray on top of the foil, so your food doesn't stick while cooking. Also, don't put little foil packets inside your pan because this could cause grease fires.

What can I cook in my air fryer?

The air fryer is a versatile kitchen appliance that can be used to cook a variety of food items. Meats such as chicken, fish, and pork can be cooked in the air fryer, as well as vegetables such as potatoes, Brussels sprouts, and carrots. Additionally, many air fryers come with an attached rotisserie, which can be used to cook evenly-sized pieces of meat. In terms of desserts, air fryers can be used to make crispy treats such as cookies and pies. Air fryers provide an alternative to deep frying that is healthier and less messy. As such, they are a valuable addition to any kitchen.

How long does it take to cook food in an air fryer?

This is one of the most popular air fryer questions, but the answer isn't as simple as it might seem. Several factors can affect cooking time, such as the type and size of the food, the air fryer model, and the desired level of doneness. In general, however, most air-fried foods will be cooked through in 10 to 15 minutes. This is much faster than traditional methods like oven-baking or deep-frying, making air fryers ideal for busy weeknight meals. So if you're wondering how long it takes to cook chicken wings or French fries in an air fryer, the answer is usually around 15 minutes. Just be sure to keep an eye on your food so it doesn't overcook!

How do I know when my food is done?

Most new models come with an automatic-shutoff timer that goes off when cooking time is finished. Another way to make sure food is done is to poke the centre of whatever you're cooking with a fork; if it comes out clean, the food is ready. Some people like their food a little more done, in which case, leave it to cook for a little longer. Lastly, pay attention to smell; if it starts burning, pull the food out immediately.

Does air-fried food contain less fat than deep-fried food?

Generally speaking, yes. Because the food is not being cooked in oil, there's less of an opportunity for the fat to be absorbed into the food. However, it's important to note that air-fried food is not necessarily fat-free. The amount of fat in air-fried food will depend on the type of food being cooked and the ingredients used.

Is air-fried food crispy?

This will depend on the type of food and ingredients being used. However, many air fryers have a built-in fan that helps to ensure that the food comes out crispy.

Notes

Here are ten things you should know about air fryers before you buy one:

- Air fryers come in different sizes; some are small enough to fit on your countertop, while others are larger and require storage space. Choose the size according to your needs.
- Air fryers have different features, so make sure to choose one that has the features you want. For instance, some air fryers have a timer, while others don't.
- Air fryers come in both electric and stovetop models. Decide which type is right for you based on your kitchen setup and cooking preferences.
- When cooking with an air fryer, preheat it before adding the food, which will help ensure that the food is cooked evenly.
- Be sure to read the manual that comes with your air fryer before using it. This will help you understand how to use it properly and avoid any safety hazards.
- When cooking meat in an air fryer, it's important to use lean cuts of meat to prevent it from drying out. Chicken breasts or pork tenderloin are good options.
- Air-fried foods can be just as unhealthy as deep-fried foods if they're not cooked properly. To ensure your food is cooked evenly, don't overcrowd the basket of your air fryer. And be sure to shake the basket periodically during cooking, so the food doesn't stick together or burn.
- Most air-fried foods are best served immediately after cooking; however, some foods, like French fries, can be reheated in the air fryer if necessary. Just be sure to follow the instructions in your manual to avoid overcooking.

4-Week Meal Plan

Week 1

Day 1:
Breakfast: Egg Potato Burrito
Lunch: Palatable Brussels Sprouts
Snack: Crispy Sweet Potato Chips
Dinner: Braised Steak
Dessert: Cinnamon Bread Pudding

Day 2:
Breakfast: Buttermilk Biscuits
Lunch: Herbed Cauliflower Florets
Snack: Crispy Pumpkin Seeds
Dinner: Pork Chops
Dessert: Blueberry Crumble

Day 3:
Breakfast: Cheese Sausage Frittata
Lunch: Vegetables & Bacon Burgers
Snack: Easy French Fries
Dinner: Flounder Fillets
Dessert: Homemade Smores

Day 4:
Breakfast: Strawberry Almonds Porridge
Lunch: Tofu Cubes
Snack: Grilled Corn
Dinner: Veggies & Chicken Breasts
Dessert: Apple Fritters

Day 5:
Breakfast: Red Potatoes & Peppers
Lunch: Green Beans and Mushrooms
Snack: Crispy Cheese Sticks
Dinner: Breaded Cod Fillets
Dessert: Pumpkin Muffins

Day 6:
Breakfast: Crumbled Sausage Pizza
Lunch: Chickpeas Falafels with Tahini Sauce
Snack: Fried Ravioli
Dinner: Whole Cooked Chicken
Dessert:

Day 7:
Breakfast: Dijon Feta Shakshuka
Lunch: Cauliflower Tacos
Snack: Tasty Crackers
Dinner: Marinated Turkey Thighs
Dessert: Cinnamon Pear Halves

Week 2

Day 1:
Breakfast: Ham Omelet with Vegetable
Lunch: Flavourful Parmesan Aubergine
Snack: Wrapped Avocado
Dinner: Pork Tenderloin with Peach Salsa
Dessert: Cinnamon Apricot

Day 2:
Breakfast: Salmon in Honey-Miso Sauce
Lunch: Mini Tofu Bites
Snack: Breaded Courgette Sticks
Dinner: Garlicky Salmon
Dessert: Vanilla Pecan Brownies

Day 3:
Breakfast: Baked Cinnamon Rolls
Lunch: Spicy Okra Fries
Snack: Exotic Chicken Meatballs
Dinner: Spiced Turkey Breast
Dessert: Butter Peanut Cookies

Day 4:
Breakfast: Easy Egg Rolls
Lunch: Onion & Sweet Potato
Snack: Mac & Cheese Balls
Dinner: Hot Fried Chicken
Dessert: Tasty Chocolate Donuts

Day 5:
Breakfast: Egg Toast Cups
Lunch: Spiced Pumpkin Pieces
Snack: Crusted Chicken Tenders
Dinner: Rib-eye Steak
Dessert: Hazelnut Chocolate Brownies

Day 6:
Breakfast: Fried Potato Pieces
Lunch: Tangy Cauliflower
Snack: Avocado Fries
Dinner: Rosemary Lamb Roast
Dessert: Cinnamon Bread Pudding

Day 7:
Breakfast: Potato Pancakes
Lunch: Golden Onion Rings
Snack: Savory Chickpeas
Dinner: BBQ Pork Ribs
Dessert: Blueberry Crumble

Week 3

Day 1:
Breakfast: Walnut Courgette Bread
Lunch: Parmesan Brussels Sprout
Snack: Crispy Pumpkin Seeds
Dinner: Beef Kebabs
Dessert: Homemade Smores

Day 2:
Breakfast: Cheese Onion Stuffed Peppers
Lunch: Cheese Stuffed Mushrooms
Snack: Easy French Fries
Dinner: Flavourful Tilapia Fillets
Dessert: Apple Fritters

Day 3:
Breakfast: Spinach Pie with Cheese
Lunch: Mini Beef Burger
Snack: Grilled Corn
Dinner: Veggies Chicken Pie
Dessert: Pumpkin Muffins

Day 4:
Breakfast: Butter Banana Bread
Lunch: Cheese Broccoli Gratin
Snack: Crispy Cheese Sticks
Dinner: Turkey Breast and Bacon
Dessert: Cinnamon Pear Halves

Day 5:
Breakfast: Buttermilk Biscuits
Lunch: Cauliflower Fritters with Parmesan
Snack: Crispy Sweet Potato Chips
Dinner: Short Beef Ribs
Dessert: Cinnamon Apricot

Day 6:
Breakfast: Egg Potato Burrito
Lunch: Simple Cheese Balls
Snack: Cheese Spinach Rolls
Dinner: Lemon Lamb Chops
Dessert: Vanilla Pecan Brownies

Day 7:
Breakfast: Red Potatoes & Peppers
Lunch: Palatable Brussels Sprouts
Snack: Crispy Potato Chips
Dinner: Peanut Butter Chicken Thighs
Dessert: Butter Peanut Cookies

Week 4

Day 1:
Breakfast: Crumbled Sausage Pizza
Lunch: Tofu Cubes
Snack: Fried Ravioli
Dinner: Simple-Seasoned Beef
Dessert: Tasty Chocolate Donuts

Day 2:
Breakfast: Dijon Feta Shakshuka
Lunch: Herbed Cauliflower Florets
Snack: Wrapped Avocado
Dinner: Tuna Cakes
Dessert: Hazelnut Chocolate Brownies

Day 3:
Breakfast: Cheese Sausage Frittata
Lunch: Chickpeas Falafels with Tahini Sauce
Snack: Tasty Crackers
Dinner: Herb Chicken Thighs
Dessert: Cinnamon Bread Pudding

Day 4:
Breakfast: Baked Cinnamon Rolls
Lunch: Green Beans and Mushrooms
Snack: Breaded Courgette Sticks
Dinner: Steak with Chimichurri Sauce
Dessert: Blueberry Crumble

Day 5:
Breakfast: Egg Toast Cups
Lunch: Cauliflower Tacos
Snack: Exotic Chicken Meatballs
Dinner: Homemade Pork Tenderloin
Dessert: Homemade Smores

Day 6:
Breakfast: Ham Omelet with Vegetable
Lunch: Flavourful Parmesan Aubergine
Snack: Avocado Fries
Dinner: Rustic Whole Chicken
Dessert: Apple Fritters

Day 7:
Breakfast: Easy Egg Rolls
Lunch: Tangy Cauliflower
Snack: Crusted Chicken Tenders
Dinner: Flavourful Leg of Lamb
Dessert: Pumpkin Muffins

Chapter 1 Breakfast Recipes

Strawberry Almonds Porridge

Prep Time: 10 minutes | **Cook Time:** 10 minutes | **Serves:** 2

305g strawberries, sliced and divided
240ml milk
80g rolled oats
4 tablespoons brown sugar
½ teaspoon ground cinnamon
½ teaspoon baking powder
4 tablespoons almonds, slivered
Pinch of salt

1. Reserve 150g of strawberries. 2. Add the remaining ingredients to the baking pan and combine well. Then allow it to sit for 10 minutes. 3. Sprinkle the reserved strawberries on top. 4. Bake the food at 175°C for 10 minutes. 5. When cooked, carefully remove it from the air fryer. 6. Serve and enjoy!

Per Serving: Calories 315; Fat 8.94g; Sodium 135mg; Carbs 65.6g; Fibre 10.8g; Sugar 29.65g; Protein 13.47g

Salmon in Honey-Miso Sauce

Prep Time: 10 minutes | **Cook Time:** 15minutes | **Serves:** 4

1 teaspoon sesame seeds
2 tablespoons miso paste
2 tablespoons mirin
1 tablespoon soy sauce
1 tablespoon minced ginger
1 teaspoon honey
1 tablespoon oil, or as needed
455g salmon fillets

1. Add sesame seeds to a saucepan and heat over medium heat. Cook them for about 2 minutes, stirring from time to time. 2. Add mirin, miso paste, ginger, and honey to a small bowl. Then add the cooked sesame seeds and stir to combine. 3. Lightly grease a baking pan with oil and line with foil. 4. Coat the salmon with miso sauce. Then transfer the salmon to the prepared baking pan, skin-side up. 5. Grill the salmon at 150°C for 10 to 15 minutes. 6. When cooked, carefully remove it from the air fryer. Serve and enjoy!

Per Serving: Calories 243; Fat 13.19g; Sodium 869mg; Carbs 5.05g; Fibre 0.7g; Sugar 2.78g; Protein 24.84g

Ham Omelet with Vegetable

Prep Time: 10 minutes | **Cook Time:** 7 minutes | **Serves:** 2

4 large eggs
85g ham, cut into small pieces
60ml milk
100g mixed vegetables (white mushrooms, green onions, red pepper)
30g mixed cheddar and mozzarella cheese
1 teaspoon freshly chopped mixed herbs (coriander and chives)
Salt and freshly ground pepper to taste

1. Whisk the eggs with milk in a mixing bowl to combine. Then add ham, mixed vegetables, salt, and ground pepper and beat together with a fork. 2. Grease the baking pan with olive oil. 3. Pour the egg mixture into the prepared pan. 4. Bake the food at 175°C for 7 minutes. 5. Top the food with the remaining cheese and mixed herbs halfway through cooking. 6. You can enjoy this dish with green salad!

Per Serving: Calories 237; Fat 13.91g; Sodium 723mg; Carbs 11.56g; Fibre 0.5g; Sugar 4.08; Protein 16.45g

Red Potatoes & Peppers

Prep Time: 15 minutes | **Cook Time:** 50 minutes | **Serves:** 4

900g red potatoes, sliced into even, 1.5cm pieces
1 red pepper
½ medium white onion
2 tablespoons extra-virgin olive oil
1 teaspoon garlic powder
½ teaspoon sea salt
Ground black pepper

1. Let the air fryer preheat at 220°C on Bake mode. 2. Add onion, pepper, and the potatoes to a rimmed baking pan, and then add 2 tablespoons oil, salt, ground black pepper, and garlic powder to season. 3. Toss to coat well and arrange in an even layer on the pan. 4. After preheating, bake the vegetables at 220°C for 45 to 50 minutes. 5. When cooked, carefully remove it from the air fryer. 6. Serve and enjoy!

Per Serving: Calories 200; Fat 3.41g; Sodium 394mg; Carbs 39.27g; Fibre 4.5g; Sugar 4.13g; Protein 4.86g

Cheese Sausage Frittata

Prep Time: 15 minutes | **Cook Time:** 20 minutes | **Serves:** 2

115g breakfast sausage
4 lightly beaten eggs
50g shredded Cheddar cheese
2 tablespoons diced red pepper
1 chopped green onion
Cooking spray
1 pinch Cayenne pepper (optional)

1. Add eggs, sausage, cheddar, Cayenne, green onion, and the chopped red pepper to a bowl, and mix them well. 2. Air-fry the mixture at 180°C for 18 to 20 minutes. 3. When cooked, carefully remove it from the air fryer. 4. Serve and enjoy!

Per Serving: Calories 552; Fat 38.29g; Sodium 1219mg; Carbs 17.89g; Fibre 1.7g; Sugar 11.87g; Protein 33.14g

Fried Potato Pieces

Prep Time: 10 minutes | **Cook Time:** 20 minutes | **Serves:** 4

3-4 russet potatoes, peel and chop into 2.5cm pieces
2-3 tablespoons olive oil
1 teaspoon salt
1 teaspoon garlic powder
½ teaspoon onion powder
½ teaspoon sweet paprika
cooking spray

1. Add the potatoes, spice, and olive oil to a large bowl and toss well to coat. 2. Spritz the cooking tray with non-stick cooking spray. Then add the potatoes to the tray. 3. Air-fry the potato pieces at 205°C for 20 minutes. 4. Toss the pieces once or more halfway through cooking. 5. When the potatoes have cooked, carefully remove them from the air fryer. 6. Serve and enjoy!

Per Serving: Calories 334; Fat 8.76g; Sodium 599mg; Carbs 59.31g; Fibre 4.4g; Sugar 2.07g; Protein 7.11g

Buttermilk Biscuits

Prep Time: 10 minutes | **Cook Time:** 5 minutes | **Serves:** 12

240g plain flour
1 tablespoon baking powder
¼ teaspoon baking soda
2 teaspoons sugar
1 teaspoon salt
6 tablespoons cold unsalted butter, cut into 1-tablespoon slices
180ml buttermilk
55g unsalted butter, melted (optional)

1. Mix baking soda, baking powder, sugar, flour, and salt in a mixing bowl. 2. Add butter for a coarse mixture. 3. Mix in buttermilk for a smooth mixture. 4. Lightly dust a clean work surface with flour and roll the dough on the surface to roll into 1 cm thick. 5. Cut the flattened dough into biscuits with a 5 cm biscuit cutter. 6. Air-fry the biscuits at 180°C for 5 minutes. 7. When cooked, carefully remove from the air fryer and transfer to a serving platter. Enjoy!

Per Serving: Calories 120; Fat 4.2g; Sodium 254mg; Carbs 17.63g; Fibre 0.6g; Sugar 1.26g; Protein 2.89g

Easy Egg Rolls

Prep Time: 10 minutes | **Cook Time:** 10 minutes | **Serves:** 4

4 eggs
Pinch of salt
Pinch of pepper
1 teaspoon butter
50g Cheddar cheese shredded
4 slices bacon cooked and crumbled
4 egg roll wrappers

1. Crack the eggs in a small mixing bowl and add salt and pepper to season. Whisk well to combine. 2. Melt the butter in the frying pan over medium heat. 3. Top with Cheddar cheese and bacon crumbles and whisk until well incorporated. 4. Lightly brush the edges of the egg rolls with water. Place ¼ of the egg mixture on the centre of the egg rolls. Fold in the left edge with the right edge, and then fold the bottom corner up. Roll the egg roll and seal the top point with more water, as needed. 5. Do the same with the remaining rolls. 6. Arrange the egg rolls evenly in the cooking tray. 7. Air-fry the egg rolls at 200°C for 8 minutes, flipping them once halfway through cooking. 8. When done, serve and enjoy!

Per Serving: Calories 342; Fat 21.43g; Sodium 521mg; Carbs 20.35g; Fibre 0.7g; Sugar 1g; Protein 16.12g

Crumbled Sausage Pizza

Prep Time: 5 minutes | **Cook Time:** 15 minutes | **Serves:** 4

Crescent dough
3 eggs, scrambled
Crumbled sausage
½ chopped pepper
50g Cheddar cheese
55g Mozzarella cheese

1. Spray the baking pan with oil. 2. Place the dough on the prepared baking pan, and evenly arrange the remaining ingredients on the dough. 3. Bake the dough at 175°C for 5 to 10 minutes. 4. When cooked, carefully remove it from the air fryer. 5. Serve and enjoy!

Per Serving: Calories 218; Fat 14.38g; Sodium 373mg; Carbs 5.19g; Fibre 0.6g; Sugar 1.04g; Protein 16.92g

Butter Banana Bread

Prep Time: 10 minutes | **Cook Time:** 30 minutes | **Serves:** 4

1 egg
3 tablespoons brown sugar
90g plain flour
1 ripe banana, mashed
½ teaspoon baking soda
60g sour cream
2 tablespoons butter, melted
¼ teaspoon salt

1. Add butter, egg, brown sugar, sour cream, and banana to a bowl and mix well. 2. Mix in baking soda, salt, and flour and combine well. 3. Lightly grease a loaf pan, and then pour in the batter. 4. Bake the loaf at 160°C for 30 minutes. 5. When the cooking time is up, carefully remove the pan from the air fryer. 6. Serve and enjoy!

Per Serving: Calories 221; Fat 8.66g; Sodium 377mg; Carbs 31.72g; Fibre 1.4g; Sugar 9.62g; Protein 4.69g

Egg Toast Cups

Prep Time: 5 minutes | **Cook Time:** 15 minutes | **Serves:** 4

1 non-stick cooking spray
4 slice whole-wheat bread (toasted)
1½ tablespoons trans-fat free tub margarine (such as I Can't Believe It's Not Butter)
1 slice (about 50g) deli-style ham, sliced into 1 cm strips
4 large eggs
⅛ teaspoon salt
⅛ teaspoon black pepper

1. Prepare 4 (200g) oven-safe custard cups or ramekins and spritz the inside with non-stick cooking spray. 2. Spread the margarine over one side of the bread and then arrange it inside a ramekin, margarine-side down. Gently press inside the cup. Repeat for the rest three. 3. Add the ham strips to the cups in a single layer and crack one egg into each cup. Add salt and pepper to season. 4. Arrange the custard cups in the baking pan. 5. Bake the eggs at 190°C for 10 to 13 minutes. 6. When the egg cups are done, carefully remove them from the air fryer and transfer the cups to a serving plate. Enjoy!

Per Serving: Calories 139; Fat 5.66g; Sodium 294mg; Carbs 16.47g; Fibre 2.1g; Sugar 0.33g; Protein 6.44g

Cauliflower Fritters

Prep Time: 10 minutes | **Cook Time:** 15 minutes | **Serves:** 8

10g chopped parsley
100g Italian breadcrumbs
40g shredded mozzarella cheese
35g shredded sharp cheddar cheese
1 egg
2 minced garlic cloves
3 chopped spring onions
1 head of cauliflower, cut into florets

1. Wash the cauliflower florets and pat them dry. 2. Add the cauliflower florets to a food processor and pulse for 20 to 30 seconds to 'rice.' 3. Add the cauliflower rice into a bowl and then add salt, cheeses, breadcrumbs, garlic, spring onions, and eggs. Mix them well. 4. Form 15 patties from the mixture, adding more breadcrumbs as needed. Finally, spritz the patties with olive oil and arrange them evenly on the baking pan in a single layer. 5. Bake the patties at 200°C for 14 minutes, flipping them once halfway through. 6. Serve and enjoy!

Per Serving: Calories 78; Fat 4g; Sodium 212mg; Carbs 4.85g; Fibre 1.2g; Sugar 1.42g; Protein 6.26g

Potato Pancakes

Prep Time: 10 minutes | **Cook Time:** 10 minutes | **Serves:** 4

1 egg
140g mashed potatoes
1 tablespoon garlic, minced
1 tablespoon chives, chopped
75g Cheddar cheese, grated
40g flour
1 potato, grated
1 teaspoon salt

1. Mix the grated potato, flour, chives, garlic, salt, egg, cheese, and mashed potatoes in a large mixing bowl. 2. Line a plate with parchment paper. 3. Make the potato mixture into 8 equal balls. Transfer them to the prepared plate, and then slightly flatten them and place them in the freezer for 15 minutes. 4. Transfer the patties to the cooking tray in the air fryer. 5. Air fry the patties at 205°C for 10 minutes. 6. Flip the patties halfway through cooking to cook the other side. 7. Carefully remove the tray from the air fryer. 8. Serve and enjoy!

Per Serving: Calories 274; Fat 11.01g; Sodium 775mg; Carbs 31.86g; Fibre 3.2g; Sugar 1.31g; Protein 12.04g

Cheese Onion Stuffed Peppers

Prep Time: 10 minutes | **Cook Time:** 15 minutes | **Serves:** 4

8 eggs
4 peppers, cut the top & remove seeds
100g Parmesan cheese, grated
¼ onion, chopped
75g bacon, cooked & chopped
Pepper
Salt

1. Arrange the chopped onion and bacon in the hollow peppers. 2. For each pepper, crack 2 eggs in and add 25g grated Parmesan cheese on top. Add salt and pepper to season. 3. Arrange the stuffed peppers in the baking pan. 4. Bake the peppers at 200°C for 15 minutes. 5. When the cooking time is up, carefully remove the pan from the air fryer. 6. Serve and enjoy!

Per Serving: Calories 318; Fat 21.71g; Sodium 930mg; Carbs 10.37g; Fibre 1.4g; Sugar 2.93g; Protein 21.41g

Spinach Pie with Cheese

Prep Time: 10 minutes | **Cook Time:** 20 minutes | **Serves:** 4

5 eggs
250g frozen spinach, squeezed & drained
60g heavy cream
100g Cheddar cheese, shredded
¼ teaspoon garlic powder
40g onion, diced
Pepper
Salt

1. Add heavy cream, pepper, salt, garlic powder, and eggs to a bowl and whisk together well. 2. Stir in cheese, onion, and spinach and combine well. 3. Prepare an oven-safe baking dish and lightly grease it with olive oil, then place the mixture in it. 4. Bake the patties at 160°C for 20 minutes. 5. When the cooking time is up, carefully remove the dish from the air fryer. 6. Serve and enjoy!

Per Serving: Calories 267; Fat 19.6g; Sodium 386mg; Carbs 5.91g; Fibre 2.4g; Sugar 1.85g; Protein 17.91g

Baked Cinnamon Rolls

Prep Time: 30 minutes | **Cook Time:** 20 minutes | **Serves:** 4

FOR The Dough:
180ml warm milk,
2¼ teaspoons active yeast
50g granulated sugar
1 egg + 1 egg yolk, room temperature
55g unsalted butter, melted
360g plain flour and more for dusting
¾ teaspoon salt
For The Filling:
135g light brown sugar
1½ tablespoons ground cinnamon
55g unsalted butter, room temperature
For The Cream Cheese Frosting:
100g cream cheese, room temperature
4 tablespoons unsalted butter, room temperature
95g icing sugar
1 teaspoon vanilla extract

1. Pour lukewarm milk into a bowl and add the active yeast. Stir well and allow it to sit for 5 minutes. 2. Add sugar, melted butter, and eggs and combine well. Add salt and the plain flour to the mixture when the dough is about to be formed. 3. Mix the dough into a ball with a stand mixer on medium and add flour as needed to avoid the ball from sticking to the bowl. 4. Transfer the dough into a greased bowl, and cover the bowl with plastic wrap and a hot towel. 5. Let the dough sit on a clean work surface for about 1 hour 30 minutes or until the dough has doubled the size. 6. Portion the dough into two, and then flatten them into one square meter with a rolling pin on a lightly floured surface. 7. Lightly rub the dough with butter and leave a small edge. 8. In a small bowl, add sugar and cinnamon and mix well. Then sprinkle over the buttered dough. Lightly press the dough. 9. Cut the flattened dough into 4 cm wide strips with a pizza cutter. Then roll the strips. 10. Arrange the cinnamon rolls evenly in the baking pan. 11. Bake the rolls at 175°C for 15 minutes. You can cook the rolls in batches. 12. Add the frosting ingredients to a medium bowl and beat together until smooth. 13. Carefully remove the pan from the air fryer. 14. Sprinkle the frosting on top, and you can serve with apple slices!

Per Serving: Calories 805; Fat 35.26g; Sodium 613mg; Carbs 105.68g; Fibre 4.7g; Sugar 28.97g; Protein 16.75g

Dijon Feta Shakshuka

Prep Time: 5 minutes | **Cook Time:** 25 minutes | **Serves:** 6

40g chopped parsley
15g chopped mint
15g chopped tarragon
35g chopped capers
1 tablespoon chopped anchovies
2 teaspoons Dijon mustard
30ml extra virgin olive oil
1 red onion
1 red pepper
3 garlic cloves
1 teaspoon cumin
1 teaspoon smoked paprika
1 teaspoon turmeric
2 cans (350g) chopped tomatoes
160g crumbled Feta
6 eggs

1. Mix the parsley, mint, anchovies, and tarragon in a bowl. Add oil and mustard to the mixture. Set aside for later use. 2. Cook the onion, peppers, and garlic in the frying pan for about 10 minutes. 3. Add the tomatoes and spices to the frying pan and simmer them for about 5 minutes. 4. Add feta and the mustard mixture. 5. Make 6 wells in the mixture with a spoon and crack an egg in each well, and then arrange them onto the baking pan. 6. Bake the burritos at 175°C for 8 minutes. 7. When cooked, carefully remove it from the air fryer. 8. You can serve the dish with sourdough bread and sprinkle some coriander.

Per Serving: Calories 296; Fat 20.62g; Sodium 801mg; Carbs 11.54g; Fibre 4.2g; Sugar 6.32g; Protein 17.33g

Egg Potato Burrito

Prep Time: 20 minutes | **Cook Time:** 20 minutes | **Serves:** 6

Tortillas
350g sausage meat
Second protein (ham, ground chicken, bacon)
300g chopped potatoes
80g red onion
75g diced peppers, red, green, and yellow
6-8 eggs
½ teaspoon salt
1 teaspoon pepper
½ teaspoon garlic powder
1 teaspoon Italian seasoning
200g shredded cheese
2 tablespoons butter
3 tablespoons olive oil

1. Add 2 tablespoons of butter and 3 tablespoons of olive oil to the pan and heat them over medium heat. 2. Add potatoes to the oil and cook for 7 to 8 minutes; add onions and peppers and cook for 3 to 4 minutes. Set aside. 3. Add the proteins and cook. Drain and remove from the pan. 4. In the same pan, scramble the eggs and lightly season them with salt and pepper. 5. In the centre of the tortilla, add scrambled eggs with a spoon and lightly mash down to hold the remaining ingredients. 6. Then add the proteins, potatoes, and veggies, and then sprinkle the cheese on top. Tightly roll the burrito. 7. Bake the burritos at 180°C for 6 minutes. 8. When cooked, carefully remove it from the air fryer. You can enjoy the dish with veggies!

Per Serving: Calories 581; Fat 40.92g; Sodium 748mg; Carbs 16.7g; Fibre 1.8g; Sugar 2.67g; Protein 7.14g

Walnut Courgette Bread

Prep Time: 10 minutes | **Cook Time:** 30 minutes | **Serves:** 10

1 egg
125g plain flour
60g shredded apple
1 teaspoon vanilla
80ml rapeseed oil
¼ teaspoon baking soda
40g walnuts, chopped
65g shredded courgette
¾ teaspoon baking powder
1¼ teaspoons cinnamon
¼ teaspoon salt

1. Mix together salt, cinnamon, baking powder, and baking soda in a bowl. 2. Whisk egg, rapeseed oil, sugar, and vanilla in a separate bowl until well mixed. 3. Mix the egg mixture and the flour mixture in the egg mixture bowl and combine well. 4. Stir in courgette, apple, and walnuts until well combined. 5. Lightly grease an oven-proof load pan. Transfer the mixture to the pan. 6. Place the pan in the air fryer, and then bake the food at 165°C for 30 minutes. 7. When the bread has baked, carefully remove it from the air fryer and let it cool for about several minutes. 8. Turn upside down the bread to a cutting board. Slice into your desired-sized slice. 9. Serve with your favored jam. Enjoy!

Per Serving: Calories 138; Fat 9.47g; Sodium 98mg; Carbs 11.2g; Fibre 0.8g; Sugar 0.75g; Protein 2.29g

Chapter 2 Snacks and Appetizers Recipes

Crispy Pumpkin Seeds

Prep Time: 10 minutes | **Cook Time:** 40 minutes | **Serves:** 4

120g pumpkin seeds, pulp removed, rinsed
1 tablespoon butter, melted
1 tablespoon brown sugar
1 teaspoon orange zest
½ teaspoon cardamom
½ teaspoon salt

1. Bake the seeds in the air fryer at 160°C for 4 minutes. 2. Add sugar, orange zest, salt, cardamom, and melted butter to a bowl and whisk them well. 3. Toss together the seeds and the cardamom mixture in the bowl to coat well. 4. Return the seeds to the air fryer. 5. Bake the seeds again at 150°C for 35 minutes or until lightly browned, tossing them lightly every 10 to 12 minutes. 6. Serve and enjoy!

Per Serving: Calories 204; Fat 17.37g; Sodium 389mg; Carbs 6.66g; Fibre 2g; Sugar 2.45g; Protein 8.87g

Easy French Fries

Prep Time: 10 minutes | **Cook Time:** 16 minutes | **Serves:** 2

225g potatoes, peeled and cut into 1cm thick sticks lengthwise
1 tablespoon olive oil
Salt and ground black pepper to taste

1. Add all of the ingredients to a large mixing bowl and toss well to coat. 2. Transfer the coated potato sticks to the cooking tray. 3. Air fry the potato sticks at 205°C for 16 minutes. 4. When done, carefully remove the tray from the air fryer. Serve and enjoy!

Per Serving: Calories 150; Fat 6.89g; Sodium 7mg; Carbs 20.55g; Fibre 2.8g; Sugar 0.89g; Protein 2.41g

Breaded Courgette Sticks

Prep Time: 30 minutes | **Cook Time:** 15 minutes | **Serves:** 4

3 medium courgette, cut into strips
Salt
50g Gluten-free breadcrumbs
15g Nutritional yeast
1 tablespoon granulated garlic
1 tablespoon dried parsley
½ teaspoon Salt
1 egg, beaten
Cooking spray
3 tablespoons Olive oil

1. Place the courgette strips on the baking pan and add salt. Allow it to sit for about 20 minutes. Then pat dry. 2. Add nutritional yeast, breadcrumbs, salt, and parsley to a mixing bowl and mix well. 3. Beat the eggs in a shallow bowl. 4. Dip the courgette stick first in the beaten eggs and then coat thoroughly with the breadcrumbs. 5. Place the coated courgette sticks inside the cooking tray, and brush the top with oil. 6. Bake the food at 205°C for 15 minutes. 7. Turn over to brush the other side halfway through. 8. Serve and enjoy!

Per Serving: Calories 174; Fat 12.83g; Sodium 913mg; Carbs 8.04g; Fibre 1.4g; Sugar 0.62g; Protein 7.22g

Crispy Cheese Sticks

Prep Time: 10 minutes | **Cook Time:** 70 minutes | **Serves:** 2

25g of mozzarella string cheese sticks, cut in half
2 large eggs
55g grated Parmesan cheese
1 teaspoon dried parsley

1. Place the sticks in a freezer and freeze overnight until they are firm. 2. Add parsley, and parmesan to a large bowl and mix well. 3. Whisk eggs in a bowl. 4. Dip the frozen mozzarella sticks first in the whisked eggs, and then coat well with the parmesan mixture. Repeat with the remaining sticks. 5. Transfer the mozzarella sticks onto the cooking tray. 6. Air fry the sticks at 205°C for 10 minutes until golden. 7. Carefully remove the tray from the air fryer. 8. Serve and enjoy!

Per Serving: Calories 199; Fat 12.73g; Sodium 569mg; Carbs 4.63g; Fibre 0.3g; Sugar 0.33g; Protein 16.1g

Crispy Potato Chips

Prep Time: 15 minutes | **Cook Time:** 25 minutes | **Serves:** 4

4 medium yellow potatoes, cut into thin slices
1 tablespoon oil
Salt to taste

1. Soak the potato slices in a bowl with cold water for at least 20 minutes. 2. Drain them and pat dry. 3. Toss the potato slice with salt and olive oil to season. 4. Place the slices in the cooking tray, and then air fry the slices at 95°C for 20 minutes. 5. When the cooking has done, toss the potato chips and continue cooking for 5 minutes at 205°C. 6. Carefully remove from the air fryer. 7. Serve and enjoy!

Per Serving: Calories 314; Fat 3.73g; Sodium 61mg; Carbs 64.46g; Fibre 8.1g; Sugar 2.88g; Protein 7.45g

Cheese Spinach Rolls

Prep Time: 15 minutes | **Cook Time:** 25 minutes | **Serves:** 4-6

175g of baby spinach
1 clove of minced garlic
250g Ricotta
35g Parmesan
100g shredded cheddar cheese
2 eggs
2 green onions
Salt & pepper to taste
Thawed frozen puff pastry, 2 sheets

1. Heat the oil in a frying pan over medium heat. 2. Add garlic and cook for 30 seconds, stirring from time to time. 3. Add spinach in the frying pan and cook for 3 minutes or more. Add salt. Set aside for later use. 4. Add Cheddar cheese, Parmesan cheese, 1 egg, green onion, and ricotta in a mixing bowl and mix in spinach. Combine well. 5. Half the puff pastry and fill the puff pastry halves with the spinach mixture. 6. Brush beaten egg liquid over sides and roll tightly into logs. 7. Place the rolls in the refrigerator for 15 minutes. 8. Then cut them into 4 pieces and brush with beaten egg liquid. 9. Place the pieces in the cooking tray, and then air fry them at 200°C for 15 to 20 minutes. 10. When the cooking time is up, carefully remove the tray from the air fryer. 11. Serve and enjoy!

Per Serving: Calories 33.; Fat 23.14g; Sodium 332mg; Carbs 13.2g; Fibre 1.2g; Sugar 1.27g; Protein 17.67g

Grilled Corn

Prep Time: 5 minutes | **Cook Time:** 10 minutes | **Serves:** 4

4 fresh ears of corn
2 to 3 teaspoons Vegetable oil
Salt and pepper to taste

1. Remove the husk of the corn. Wash them and pat them dry. 2. Brush the corn with vegetable oil and season with salt and pepper. 3. Grill the food at 205°C for 10 minutes. 4. When the cooking time is up, carefully remove the food from the air fryer. 5. Serve and enjoy!

Per Serving: Calories 143; Fat 3.96g; Sodium 21mg; Carbs 27.21g; Fibre 3.9g; Sugar 4.6g; Protein 4.61g

Crusted Chicken Tenders

Prep Time: 10 minutes | **Cook Time:** 10 minutes | **Serves:** 4

300g chicken breasts
1 egg white
15g flour
135g Panko breadcrumbs
Salt and pepper

1. Remove the fat parts from the chicken breast and chip them into tenders. 2. Toss the chicken tender with salt and pepper to season evenly. 3. Dip the chicken tenders first in flour, then in the egg whites. Finally, coat with the Panko breadcrumbs. 4. Spray the cooking tray with olive oil and evenly arrange the chicken tenders inside the cooking tray. 5. Air fry the chicken at 175°C for 10 minutes. 6. Carefully remove the tray from the air fryer after cooking. 7. Serve and enjoy!

Per Serving: Calories 205; Fat 8.43g; Sodium 176mg; Carbs 10.66g; Fibre 0.7g; Sugar 1.42g; Protein 20.4g

Savory Chickpeas

Prep Time: 5 minutes | **Cook Time:** 20 minutes | **Serves:** 8

1 (375g) can of chickpeas - drained but not rinsed and save the liquid from the can
1 tablespoon olive oil
4 teaspoons dried dill
2 teaspoons garlic powder
2 teaspoons onion powder
¾ teaspoon sea salt
1 tablespoon lemon juice

1. Add 1 tablespoon of the reserved liquid from the chickpea can in a mixing bowl and the chickpeas and toss well. 2. Add the chickpeas as well as the liquid to the baking pan. 3. Roast the chickpeas at 205°C for 12 minutes. 4. When the cooking has done, transfer the chickpeas back to the small bowl and add olive oil, garlic powder, dill, salt, lemon juice, and onion powder. Toss to coat the beans evenly. 5. Adjust the temperature to 175°C and time to 5 minutes. 6. Roast them again in your air fryer. 7. When the cooking time is up, carefully remove the pan from the air fryer. 8. Serve and enjoy!

Per Serving: Calories 50; Fat 3.66g; Sodium 220mg; Carbs 3.32g; Fibre 0.4g; Sugar 0.11g; Protein 1.38g

Avocado Fries

Prep Time: 10 minutes | **Cook Time:** 20 minutes | **Serves:** 4

55g Panko breadcrumbs
½ teaspoon salt
1 Hass avocado peeled, pitted, and sliced
Aquafaba from a 375g can of white beans or chickpeas

1. In a small bowl, add salt and breadcrumbs and toss them together. 2. Half fill a separate bowl with aquafaba and dredge in avocado slices. 3. Then add the avocado fries to the Panko breadcrumbs and press to coat evenly. 4. Arrange the avocado fries onto the cooking tray. 5. Air fry the fries at 200°C for 10 minutes, tossing them once halfway through cooking. 6. When the cooking time is up, carefully remove the tray from the air fryer. 7. Serve and enjoy!

Per Serving: Calories 184; Fat 11.48g; Sodium 395mg; Carbs 16.98g; Fibre 4.1g; Sugar 1.17g; Protein 4.72g

Tasty Crackers

Prep Time: 25 minutes | **Cook Time:** 11 minutes | **Serves:** 4-5

300g plain flour
60g white whole wheat flour
1 teaspoon salt
180ml water
60ml plus 1 tablespoon olive oil
1 to 2 tablespoons minced fresh thyme
¾ teaspoon sea salt

1. Add flour and salt to a large bowl and whisk well. 2. Gradually add water and 60ml oil and toss until a firm dough has formed. 3. Divide the dough into three portions. 4. Knead the dough into a ½ cm thick and cut with a 2.5 cm round cookie cutter. 5. Place them in the baking pan. 6. Prick each cracker with a fork and brush lightly with the rest oil. 7. Sprinkle thyme and sea salt over the crackers. 8. Bake them at 190°C for 9 to 11 minutes. 9. When done, serve and enjoy!

Per Serving: Calories 202; Fat 5.08g; Sodium 908mg; Carbs 33.51g; Fibre 1.2g; Sugar 0.12g; Protein 4.59g

Wrapped Avocado

Prep Time: 10 minutes | **Cook Time:** 20 minutes | **Serves:** 4-6

2 medium ripe avocados
12 bacon strips
Sauce:
120g Mayonnaise
2 to 3 tablespoons Sriracha chili sauce
1 to 2 tablespoons Lime juice
1 teaspoon grated lime zest

1. Peel the avocado and remove their pits. Cut them into half, and then cut each half into three wedges. 2. Wrap each wedge with a bacon strip. 3. Place the wrapped wedges evenly inside the cooking tray in a single layer. 4. Bake the wedges at 205°C for 15 minutes. 5. While the wedges are cooking, make the sauce mixing mayonnaise, lime juice, and lime zest. 6. Carefully remove the tray from the air fryer and transfer to a serving plate. 7. Serve the mayo-lime sauce.

Per Serving: Calories 209; Fat 19.15g; Sodium 382mg; Carbs 8.37g; Fibre 5.3g; Sugar 1.27g; Protein 3.75g

Crispy Sweet Potato Chips

Prep Time: 10 minutes | **Cook Time:** 10 minutes | **Serves:** 4

1 small sweet potato, cut into 1 cm-thick slices
2 tablespoons olive oil
2 teaspoons ground cinnamon

1. Toss the potato slices and olive oil together in a bowl until the slices are well coated. 2. Stir in cinnamon and combine well. 3. Add the sweet potato to the cooking tray. 4. Air fry the sweet potato chips at 200°C for 8 minutes. 5. Stir them halfway through cooking. 6. Carefully remove the tray from the air fryer. Let the chips cool for about 5 minutes. 7. Serve and enjoy!

Per Serving: Calories 76; Fat 6.79g; Sodium 6mg; Carbs 4.15g; Fibre 1.2g; Sugar 1g; Protein 0.35g

Fried Ravioli

Prep Time: 5 minutes | **Cook Time:** 10 minutes | **Serves:** 1

12 frozen ravioli
120ml buttermilk
50g Italian breadcrumbs

1. In a bowl, add buttermilk. Then, in a separate bowl, add breadcrumbs. 2. Dip the ravioli first in the buttermilk and then in the breadcrumbs. 3. Arrange the ravioli evenly in the cooking tray. 4. Air fry them at 205°C for 7 minutes, spraying them with oil halfway through. 5. When done, serve and enjoy!

Per Serving: Calories 389; Fat 12.72g; Sodium 1198mg; Carbs 52.85; Fibre 5.4g; Sugar 13.32g; Protein 16.16g

Exotic Chicken Meatballs

Prep Time: 10 minutes | **Cook Time:** 10 minutes | **Serves:** 4

120g sweet chili sauce
2 tablespoons lime juice
2 tablespoons ketchup
1 teaspoon soy sauce
1 large egg, lightly beaten
80g Panko bread crumbs
1 finely chopped green onion
1 tablespoon minced fresh coriander
½ teaspoon salt
½ teaspoon garlic powder
455g lean chicken mince

1. Add chili sauce, soy sauce, ketchup, and lime juice to a small bowl. 2. Mix egg, coriander, green onion, garlic powder, the remaining chili sauce, and breadcrumbs in a large bowl. 3. Then add chicken and combine well. Make the mixture into 12 balls. 4. Evenly arrange the meatballs into the cooking tray in a single layer. 5. Air fry the meatballs at 175°C for 10 minutes. 6. Cook and turn them halfway. 7. Carefully remove the tray from the air fryer. 8. Serve and enjoy!

Per Serving: Calories 249; Fat 10.98g; Sodium 950mg; Carbs 14.82g; Fibre 2.6g; Sugar 6.89g; Protein 22.34g

Mac & Cheese Balls

Prep Time: 15 minutes | **Cook Time:** 20 minutes | **Serves:** 4

110g Panko breadcrumbs
535g prepared macaroni and cheese, refrigerated
3 tablespoons flour
1 teaspoon salt, divided
1 teaspoon ground black pepper, divided
1 teaspoon smoked paprika, divided
½ teaspoon garlic powder, divided
2 eggs
1 tablespoon milk
60g ranch dressing, garlic aioli, or chipotle mayo for dipping, optional

1. On a baking sheet, add the breadcrumbs and shake them to an even layer. 2. Place the baking sheet in the air fryer. 3. Bake them at 190°C for 5 minutes; after 3 minutes of cooking time, toss them and then resume cooking until the crumbs are completely toasted. 4. Make the prepared macaroni and cheese into medium-sized balls. Then arrange onto the baking sheet. 5. Add ½ teaspoon of salt, ½ teaspoon of black pepper, ½ teaspoon of smoked paprika, ¼ teaspoon of garlic powder, and flour in a suitable bowl and whisk together. 6. In a shallow bowl, add 2 eggs and milk and whisk well. 7. Toss the bread crumbs with salt, paprika, garlic powder, and pepper. 8. Dip the mac and cheese balls in the flour mixture and coat well. Then drop in the egg mixture, rolling to coat. Finally, coat with the breadcrumbs, patting to coat well. 9. Spritz the Pizza Rack with cooking spray. Arrange the mar and cheese balls evenly inside the Pizza. 10. Rack and spritz the balls with cooking spray. 11. Air fry the balls at 190°C for 10 minutes or until they are golden brown and crispy. 12. Do the same with the remaining balls. 13. When done, serve and enjoy!

Per Serving: Calories 452; Fat 3.99g; Sodium 331mg; Carbs 626g; Fibre 3.99g; Sugar 3.2g; Protein 17.48g

Chapter 3 Vegetables and Sides Recipes

Palatable Brussels Sprouts

Prep Time: 10 minutes | **Cook Time:** 20 minutes | **Serves:** 4

455g Brussels sprouts, cut in half
1 teaspoon rapeseed oil
1 tablespoon garlic, minced
3 teaspoons lime juice for serving
2 tablespoons sweet chili sauce for serving
Pepper
Salt

1. Add the Brussels sprouts to the baking pan, and then toss them with the oil, garlic, salt, and pepper. 2. Air fry the Brussels sprouts at 205°C for 20 minutes. 3. Stir the Brussels sprouts halfway through. 4. When cooked, transfer the Brussels sprouts to the bowl, add the sweet chili sauce and lime juice to the bowl and toss them well.

Per Serving: Calories 76; Fat 1.48g; Sodium 100mg; Carbs 14.53g; Fibre 4.4g; Sugar 4.22g; Protein 4.01g

Spicy Okra Fries

Prep Time: 10 minutes | **Cook Time:** 15 minutes | **Serves:** 4

375g okra, wash & pat dry
½ teaspoon garlic powder
1 teaspoon chili powder
2 tablespoons rapeseed oil
1 teaspoon paprika
Pepper
Salt

1. Mix up all the ingredients in the bowl to coat the okra well. 2. Place the coated okra in the baking pan. 3. Air fry the food at 205°C for 15 minutes. 4. Toss the okra halfway through. 5. Serve warm.

Per Serving: Calories 102; Fat 7.38g; Sodium 66mg; Carbs 8.87g; Fibre 3.9g; Sugar 1.69g; Protein 2.29g

Herbed Cauliflower Florets

Prep Time: 10 minutes | **Cook Time:** 10 minutes | **Serves:** 4

1 medium head cauliflower, cut into florets
4 tablespoons olive oil, divided
10g minced fresh parsley
1 tablespoon minced fresh rosemary
1 tablespoon chopped fresh thyme
1 teaspoon grated lemon zest
2 tablespoons lemon juice
½ teaspoon salt
¼ teaspoon crushed red pepper flakes

1. Add the cauliflower florets to a large bowl and then evenly coat them with 2 tablespoons of olive oil. 2. Arrange the cauliflower florets in batches in a single layer on the baking pan. 3. Air fry the cauliflower florets at 175°C for 10 minutes. 4. Stir them halfway through and cook until the florets are tender and the edges are browned. 5. While cooking the cauliflower florets, mix up the remaining ingredients in a bowl. 6. Transfer the cooked cauliflower florets to the serving plate, drizzle them with the mixture and toss them to combine.

Per Serving: Calories 142; Fat 13.78g; Sodium 313mg; Carbs 4.65g; Fibre 1.7g; Sugar 1.67g; Protein 1.52g

Green Beans and Mushrooms

Prep Time: 15 minutes | **Cook Time:** 20 minutes | **Serves:** 6

455g fresh green beans, cut into 5cm pieces
225g sliced fresh mushrooms
1 small red onion, halved and thinly sliced
2 tablespoons olive oil
1 teaspoon Italian seasoning
¼ teaspoon salt
⅛ teaspoon pepper

1. Grease the baking pan with oil or cooking spray. 2. Add all the ingredients to a large bowl and then toss them to coat the green beans well. 3. Arrange the food in the baking pan. 4. Air fry them at 190°C for 20 minutes, tossing halfway through. 5. Serve warm.

Per Serving: Calories 71; Fat 4.99g; Sodium 136mg; Carbs 5.9g; Fibre 2.1g; Sugar 1.89g; Protein 2.17g

Onion & Sweet Potato

Prep Time: 10 minutes | **Cook Time:** 30 minutes | **Serves:** 4

4 sweet potatoes, peel & dice
100g mushrooms, sliced
2 tablespoons fresh lemon juice
75g pepper, chopped
80g onion, chopped
½ teaspoon dried rosemary
2 tablespoons rapeseed oil
½ teaspoon dried thyme
Pepper
Salt

1. Toss the diced sweet potatoes with the remaining ingredients in a bowl and then arrange them in the baking pan. 2. Bake the sweet potatoes at 180°C for 30 minutes. 3. Toss them halfway through cooking. 4. Serve warm.

Per Serving: Calories 240; Fat 7.23g; Sodium 51mg; Carbs 41g; Fibre 3.2g; Sugar 2.44g; Protein 4.91g

Flavourful Parmesan Aubergine

Prep Time: 20 minutes | **Cook Time:** 10 minutes | **Serves:** 4

1 large aubergine mine was around 575g
50g whole wheat bread crumbs
3 tablespoons finely grated Parmesan cheese
Salt to taste
1 teaspoon Italian seasoning mix
3 tablespoons whole wheat flour
1 egg + 1 tablespoon of water
Olive oil spray
240g marinara sauce
30g grated Mozzarella cheese
Fresh parsley or basil to garnish

1. Cut the aubergine into 1 cm slices. 2. Season the aubergine slices with salt on both sides and let them sit for 10 to 15 minutes. 3. Combine the flour, egg, and water in the bowl to make the batter. 4. Mix up the bread crumbs, Parmesan cheese, Italian seasoning blend, and salt in another bowl. 5. Coat the aubergine slices with the batter and then dip them in the breadcrumb mixture. 6. Spray breaded aubergine slices with oil and place them on the baking pan. 7. Air fry the aubergine slices at 180°C for 10 minutes. 8. After 8 minutes of cooking time, top the aubergine pieces with about one tablespoon of marinara sauce and fresh mozzarella cheese, then resume cooking them. 9. When the time is up, transfer them to the serving plate or bowl.

Per Serving: Calories 169; Fat 3.3g; Sodium 787mg; Carbs 27.46g; Fibre 6.7g; Sugar 8.48g; Protein 9.61g

Tofu Cubes

Prep Time: 5 minutes | **Cook Time:** 25 minutes | **Serves:** 4

400g firm tofu, pressed and cubed
1 tablespoon vegan oyster sauce
1 tablespoon tamari sauce
1 teaspoon cider vinegar
1 teaspoon pure maple syrup
1 teaspoon sriracha
½ teaspoon shallot powder
½ teaspoon porcini powder
1 teaspoon garlic powder
1 tablespoon sesame oil
2 tablespoons golden flaxseed meal

1. Mix the tofu with the remaining ingredients in a bowl and then allow the tofu to marinate for 30 minutes. 2. Place the coated tofu in the baking pan. 3. Bake the tofu cubes at 185°C for 22 minutes. 4. After 10 minutes of cooking time, flip the food and cook for 12 minutes longer. 5. When done, serve and enjoy.

Per Serving: Calories 233; Fat 15.49g; Sodium 182mg; Carbs 8.94g; Fibre 4.2g; Sugar 1.35g; Protein 19.12g

Spiced Pumpkin Pieces

Prep Time: 10 minutes | **Cook Time:** 15 minutes | **Serves:** 4

560g squash, cut into pieces
¼ teaspoon dried thyme
¼ teaspoon dried oregano
1 tablespoon parsley, minced
1 tablespoon rapeseed oil
1 teaspoon garlic, minced
Pepper
Salt

1. Toss the squash pieces with the remaining ingredients in a bowl and transfer them to the baking pan. 2. Bake the squash pieces at 190°C for 15 minutes. 3. Stir the squash pieces halfway through cooking. 4. Serve warm.

Per Serving: Calories 33; Fat 3.52g; Sodium 39mg; Carbs 0.37g; Fibre 0.1g; Sugar 0.02g; Protein 0.08g

Cheese Broccoli Gratin

Prep Time: 5 minutes | **Cook Time:** 15 minutes | **Serves:** 2

80ml fat-free Milk
1 tablespoon all-purpose or gluten-free flour
½ tablespoon olive oil
½ teaspoon ground sage
¼ teaspoon salt
⅛ teaspoon freshly ground black pepper
175g roughly chopped broccoli florets
6 tablespoons shredded Cheddar cheese
2 tablespoons panko bread crumbs
1 tablespoon grated Parmesan cheese
Olive oil spray

1. Prepare an oven-safe baking dish and spray with olive oil. 2. Add milk, flour, salt, sage, pepper, and olive oil to a medium mixing bowl. Whisk well. 3. Add the broccoli to the mixture and then transfer the mixture to the baking dish. 4. Add the bread crumbs, Cheddar cheese, and Parmesan cheese to the baking dish and toss well. 5. Place the baking dish inside the baking pan. 6. Bake the food at 185°C for 14 minutes until it is golden brown on top. 7. Carefully remove the dish from the air fryer. 8. Serve and enjoy!

Per Serving: Calories 206; Fat 10.67g; Sodium 985mg; Carbs 16.39g; Fibre 1.6g; Sugar 5.81g; Protein 11.72g

Tangy Cauliflower

Prep Time: 20 minutes | **Cook Time:** 15 minutes | **Serves:** 3

1 medium head cauliflower
2 teaspoons avocado oil
3 tablespoons red hot sauce
2 tablespoons nutritional yeast
1½ teaspoons maple syrup
¼ teaspoon sea salt
1 tablespoon cornflour

1. In a mixing bowl, add avocado oil, red hot sauce, nutritional yeast, maple syrup, sea salt, and cornflour, and mix well to combine. 2. Then add the coated cauliflower to the bowl and evenly coat with the mixture. 3. Add the cauliflower to an oven-safe baking dish. 4. Air fry the cauliflower at 185°C for 25 minutes. 5. You can store the left the cauliflower in the refrigerator until firmly wrapped, about 3 to 4 days. 6. Air fry them in the air fryer for 1 to 2 minutes to reheat until crispy. 7. Serve and enjoy!

Per Serving: Calories 93; Fat 3.45g; Sodium 580mg; Carbs 12.05g; Fibre 2.7g; Sugar 4.24g; Protein 4.7g

Golden Onion Rings

Prep Time: 5 minutes | **Cook Time:** 20 minutes | **Serves:** 3

45g almond flour
180ml coconut milk
1 big white onion, sliced into rings
1 egg, beaten
1 tablespoon baking powder
1 tablespoon smoked paprika
Salt and pepper to taste

1. In a medium mixing bowl, add the baking powder, smoked paprika, salt, pepper, and almond flour and mix well. 2. In a separate small bowl, whisk the eggs and coconut milk together. 3. Soak the onion rings in the egg mixture. Then coat them with the flour mixture. 4. Evenly arrange the coated onion rings onto the cooking tray. 5. Air fry the onion rings at 205°C for 15 minutes. 6. Cook and turn the onion rings to the other side halfway through cooking. 7. Carefully remove the tray from the air fryer and transfer to a serving plate. 8. Serve and enjoy!

Per Serving: Calories 207; Fat 16.2g; Sodium 45mg; Carbs 15.39g; Fibre 3.2g; Sugar 7.84g; Protein 4.47g

Parmesan Brussels Sprout

Prep Time: 5 minutes | **Cook Time:** 16 minutes | **Serves:** 2

2 tablespoons Parmesan, freshly grated
225g Brussels sprouts, thinly sliced
1 teaspoon garlic powder
1 tablespoon extra-virgin olive oil
Caesar dressing for dipping
Freshly ground black pepper to taste
Salt to taste

1. Add oil, garlic powder, Parmesan cheese, and Brussels sprouts to a large mixing bowl and toss together. 2. Season with salt and pepper. 3. Evenly arrange the coated Brussels sprouts into the baking pan. 4. Air fry the Brussels sprouts at 185°C for 16 minutes until the Brussels sprouts are crispy and golden brown, and toss from time to time while cooking. 5. When the cooking time is up, carefully remove the pan from the air fryer and transfer the food to a serving plate. 6. Sprinkle the dish with Parmesan cheese. 7. Serve and enjoy!

Per Serving: Calories 100; Fat 3.6g; Sodium 224mg; Carbs 13.31g; Fibre 4.5g; Sugar 2.61g; Protein 6.12g

Cauliflower Tacos

Prep Time: 25 minutes | **Cook Time:** 70 minutes | **Serves:** 4

For The Slaw
90g thinly sliced red cabbage
½ small red onion, diced
1 jalapeño, minced
1 clove of garlic, minced
Juice of 1 lime
2 tablespoons apple cider vinegar
Pinch of salt

For The Cauliflower
125g plain flour
1 teaspoon chili powder
1 teaspoon cumin
½ teaspoon garlic powder
½ teaspoon cayenne pepper
Salt
Freshly ground black pepper
240ml almond milk or other non-dairy milk
110g Panko breadcrumbs
1 medium head cauliflower, cut into bite-size florets
Cooking spray

For Serving
120g vegan mayonnaise
2 tablespoons Sriracha
1 teaspoon maple syrup
Corn tortillas
Sliced avocado
Freshly chopped coriander
Lime wedges

1. Mix up all the slaw ingredients in a bowl, then allow the mixture to sit while preparing tacos, stirring occasionally. 2. Combine the flour, cumin, chili powder, garlic powder, cayenne pepper, salt, and pepper in the second bowl, and stir in the almond milk until the mixture is thick but not too thick. 3. Add the Panko to the third bowl. 4. Dip the florets into the milk mixture, wiping off any excess, then into the Panko. 5. Spray the covered cauliflower with cooking spray and place them in the baking pan. 6. Air fry the food at 205°C for 15 minutes. 7. Toss the cauliflower halfway through and spray with extra cooking spray. 8. Mix up the vegan mayonnaise, sriracha, and maple syrup in a small bowl. 9. Place the cauliflower, avocado, pickled slaw, coriander, and a drizzle of sriracha mayo on the top of the tortilla. 10. Serve with lime wedges.

Per Serving: Calories 449; Fat 18g; Sodium 557mg; Carbs 63.49g; Fibre 8.9g; Sugar 10.88g; Protein 11.82g

Simple Cheese Balls

Prep Time: 10 minutes | **Cook Time:** 10 minutes | **Serves:** 12

100g cream cheese
40g shredded mozzarella cheese
35g shredded cheddar cheese
2 jalapeños, finely chopped
50g bread crumbs
2 eggs
60g plain flour
Salt
Pepper
Cooking oil

1. In a medium mixing bowl, add the mozzarella, jalapenos, cheddar, and cream cheese and mix until well combined. 2. Form the mixture into 2.5 cm thick balls. Place the balls into a baking sheet and then freeze in the freezer for about 15 minutes. 3. Spray cooking spray over the cooking tray. 4. In a bowl, add the breadcrumbs. 5. In another bowl, beat the eggs. 6. In the third bowl, add flour, pepper, and salt and whisk well. 7. Dip the frozen balls first in the flour, then in the eggs, and coat with the breadcrumbs, pressing to coat well. 8. Place the balls onto the baking pan. 9. Air fry the balls at 205°C for 8 minutes, turning them halfway through cooking. 10. Carefully remove the pan from the air fryer after cooking. 11. Serve and enjoy!

Per Serving: Calories 83; Fat 4.74g; Sodium 119mg; Carbs 5.95g; Fibre 0.4g; Sugar 0.89g; Protein 4.27g

Mini Tofu Bites

Prep Time: 35 minutes | **Cook Time:** 15 minutes | **Serves:** 4

325g of extra-firm tofu
120g Franks hot sauce
60g chickpea flour
½ teaspoon garlic powder
Salt to taste
110g Panko breadcrumbs
40g rice flour
Few tablespoons of water to make a thick batter
Oil spray

1. Drain the tofu and wrap it in paper towels, then lay a heavy item on top. Press the tofu for about 30 minutes. 2. Combine the chickpea flour, garlic powder, and salt in the mixing bowl; mix in a little water until the consistency of the coating is similar to that of the pancake batter. 3. Put the breadcrumbs in another bowl. 4. Cut the pressed tofu into sticks or nugget-sized pieces. 5. Coat the tofu pieces in the rice flour, then in the chickpea flour batter, and lastly, coat them with the breadcrumbs. 6. Arrange the coated tofu pieces in the baking pan. 7. Air fry the tofu pieces at 205°C for 15 minutes. 8. Turn the tofu pieces halfway through. 9. You can cook the tofu pieces in batches.

Per Serving: Calories 255; Fat 7.55g; Sodium 432mg; Carbs 33.1g; Fibre 3.6g; Sugar 4.34g; Protein 15.67g

Chickpeas Falafels with Tahini Sauce

Prep Time: 10 minutes | **Cook Time:** 35 minutes | **Serves:** 20

½ medium yellow onion, cut into quarters
4 cloves garlic
5g packed parsley leaves
5g packed coriander leaves
2 (375g) cans chickpeas, rinsed and drained
1 teaspoon salt
1 teaspoon baking powder
1 teaspoon dried coriander
½ teaspoon crushed red pepper flakes
For Tahini Sauce
80g tahini
Juice of ½ a lemon
3 tablespoon water, plus more as needed
Pinch of salt
Pinch of red pepper flakes

1. Put the onion, garlic, parsley, and coriander into the food processor and then pulse them until coarsely chopped, scraping down edges as required. 2. Add the chickpeas, baking powder, coriander, cumin, red pepper flakes, and salt, and pulse until the chickpeas are mostly broken done but still have a few pieces. 3. Scoop out about two tablespoons of the mixture and gently roll it into a ball. Do the same with the remaining mixture. 4. Arrange them in the baking pan. 5. Air fry the falafels at 185°C for 15 minutes. 6. While cooking the falafels, combine the tahini and lemon juice in the bowl; stir in the water until the tahini mixture is completely mixed, one tablespoon at a time. 7. Add the salt and red pepper flakes to the tahini mixture. 8. Serve the falafels with tahini sauce.

Per Serving: Calories 57; Fat 2.74g; Sodium 182mg; Carbs 6.66g; Fibre 1.9g; Sugar 1.21g; Protein 2.34g

Cauliflower Fritters with Parmesan

Prep Time: 10 minutes | **Cook Time:** 15 minutes | **Serves:** 8

10g chopped parsley
100g Italian breadcrumbs
40g shredded mozzarella cheese
35g shredded sharp cheddar cheese
1 egg
2 minced garlic cloves
3 chopped spring onions
1 head of cauliflower, cut into florets

1. Rinse the cauliflower and then pat them dry. 2. Transfer to a food processor and pulse until the cauliflower resembles rice. 3. Add the cauliflower rice, parsley, breadcrumbs, mozzarella cheese, cheddar cheese, egg, garlic, and spring onions to a mixing bowl. Mix well. 4. Make the mixture into 15 patties and add some extra breadcrumbs as needed. 5. Spray olive oil over the patties and place them onto the cooking tray. 6. Bake the patties at 205°C for 14 minutes. 7. When the patties are cooked, carefully remove the tray from the air fryer. 8. Serve and enjoy!

Per Serving: Calories 78; Fat 4g; Sodium 212mg; Carbs 4.85g; Fibre 1.2g; Sugar 1.42g; Protein 6.26g

Cheese Stuffed Mushrooms

Prep Time: 5 minutes | **Cook Time:** 10 minutes | **Serves:** 3

3 Portobello mushrooms
1 teaspoon garlic
1 medium onion
3 tablespoons grated mozzarella cheese
2 slices of chopped ham
1 tomato
Green pepper
½ teaspoon sea salt
¼ teaspoon pepper
1 tablespoon olive oil

1. Finely chop or dice the tomato, pepper, onion, ham, and garlic and combine them in a bowl. 2. Wash the mushrooms and pat dry. Remove the stems from the mushrooms and drizzle them with oil. 3. Fill the mushroom caps with the tomato-ham mixture. Arrange the mushroom caps in the cooking tray. 4. Bake the mushroom caps at 205°C for 8 minutes. 5. When the cooking time is up, carefully remove the tray from the air fryer. 6. Serve and enjoy!

Per Serving: Calories 134; Fat 8.48g; Sodium 838mg; Carbs 8.94g; Fibre 1.6g; Sugar 4.88g; Protein 6.8g

Chapter 4 Fish and Seafood Recipes

Breaded Cod Fillets

Prep Time: 15 minutes | **Cook Time:** 15 minutes | **Serves:** 2

455g cod fillets
110g panko bread crumbs
1 large egg beaten
¼ teaspoon garlic salt
¼ teaspoon onion powder
¼ teaspoon fresh parsley, chopped
Olive oil spray

1. In a bowl, add the panko bread crumbs, and in another bowl, mix the egg with the garlic salt, onion powder, and parsley. 2. Dip the cod fillets into the egg mix and then into the panko bread crumbs, covering them lightly in bread crumbs. 3. Spray each piece of cod with cooking spray and arrange the cod fillets on the baking pan. 4. Bake the fillets at 205°C for 15 minutes. 5. You can serve when the cod filets are golden brown and flake easily.

Per Serving: Calories 190; Fat 3.25g; Sodium 700mg; Carbs 1.5g; Fibre 0.1g; Sugar 0.14g; Protein 36.19g

Chili Tilapia

Prep Time: 5 minutes | **Cook Time:** 10 minutes | **Serves:** 2

300g tilapia fillets
2 teaspoons chili powder
1 teaspoon cumin
1 teaspoon garlic powder
½ teaspoon oregano
½ teaspoon sea salt
¼ teaspoon ground black pepper
Zest from 1 lime
Juice of ½ lime

1. Pat dry the tilapia fillets. 2. Combine all the ingredients except for the fish and the lime juice in the bowl. 3. Coat the fish with the spice mix on all sides. 4. Place the fish in the baking pan. 5. Roast the fish at 175°C for 10 minutes. 6. When done, transfer the fish to the serving plate.

Per Serving: Calories 191; Fat 3.57g; Sodium 751mg; Carbs 6.42g; Fibre 1.5g; Sugar 1.11g; Protein 35.24g

Panko-Crusted Prawn

Prep Time: 15 minutes | **Cook Time:** 15 minutes | **Serves:** 4

455g uncooked large prawn (25 to 30), thawed if frozen
60g plain flour
1 teaspoon seasoning salt
2 large eggs
160g panko breadcrumbs
Cooking spray

1. Peel and devein the prawn (optional) and set the prawn aside for later use. 2. In a mixing bowl, mix up the plain flour and seasoning salt in a shallow dish or bowl. 3. Lightly beat the eggs in a second bowl and add the panko breadcrumbs in a third bowl. 4. Dip the prawn in the flour mixture and then dip in the egg. Let the excess egg drip back into the bowl; lastly, coat the prawn entirely in the panko. 5. Place the coated prawn onto the cooking tray. 6. Air fry the food at 175°C for 15 minutes. 7. When the prawn has cooked, let it cool for 5 minutes before serving.

Per Serving: Calories 333; Fat 5.82g; Sodium 1555mg; Carbs 42.29g; Fibre 2.2g; Sugar 2.65g; Protein 25.59g

Lemon-Flavored Salmon

Prep Time: 5 minutes | **Cook Time:** 20 minutes | **Serves:** 4

900g – 1.8kg salmon fillet
1 tablespoon fresh lemon juice
2 tablespoons Cajun seasoning blend

1. Arrange the salmon fillets on the baking pan; drizzle the fillets with the lemon juice, and season with the Cajun blend. 2. Place the fillets in the baking pan. 3. Roast the fries at 175°C for 20 minutes. 4. When done, serve warm.

Per Serving: Calories 441; Fat 20.56g; Sodium 1227mg; Carbs 2.97g; Fibre 0.6g; Sugar 0.65g; Protein 57.09g

Flavourful Tilapia Fillets

Prep Time: 5 minutes | **Cook Time:** 20 minutes | **Serves:** 2

300g tilapia fillets or other white fish (2 filets: 150g each)
½ teaspoon garlic powder
½ teaspoon lemon-pepper seasoning
½ teaspoon onion powder (optional)
Salt or sea salt, to taste
Fresh cracked black pepper, to taste
Fresh chopped parsley for garnish
Lemon wedges, to serve

1. Rinse the tilapia fillets and then use the paper towel to dry them; coat them with olive oil and season with garlic powder, lemon-pepper seasoning, onion powder (optional), salt, and black pepper on both sides. 2. Place the fish in the baking pan in a single layer. 3. Air fry the fillets at 175°C for 20 minutes. 4. When cooked, serve and enjoy with the lemon wedges.

Per Serving: Calories 301; Fat 16.49g; Sodium 206mg; Carbs 4.9g; Fibre 1.4g; Sugar 0.97g; Protein 32.66g

Rosemary Salmon

Prep Time: 15 minutes | **Cook Time:** 25 minutes | **Serves:** 6

900g side of salmon, boneless
5 sprigs of fresh rosemary
2 small lemons, divided
2 tablespoons extra virgin olive oil
1 teaspoon salt
¼ teaspoon ground black pepper
4 cloves garlic, peeled and roughly chopped

1. Line the baking pan with a piece of aluminum foil. 2. Lightly coat the foil with baking spray, then arrange two sprigs of the rosemary down the middle. 3. Cut one of the lemons into thin slices and arrange half the pieces down the middle with the rosemary. 4. Place the salmon on top. 5. Drizzle the salmon with olive oil and season with salt and pepper. Rub to coat, then scatter the garlic cloves over the top. 6. Place the remaining rosemary and lemon slices on top of the salmon. Juice the second lemon, then pour the juice over the top. 7. Fold the sides of the aluminum foil up and over the top of the salmon until it's completely enclosed. 8. Leave a little room inside the foil for air to circulate. 9. Bake the salmon at 190°C for 20 minutes. 10. When the time is up, the salmon should be almost completely cooked through at the thickest part. 11. Grill the salmon at 150°C for 3 minutes until the top of the salmon and the garlic are slightly golden, and the fish is cooked through.

Per Serving: Calories 257; Fat 12.93g; Sodium 1083mg; Carbs 1.95g; Fibre 0.2g; Sugar 0.42g; Protein 31.42g

Red Snapper with Lemon Slices

Prep Time: 10 minutes | **Cook Time:** 10 minutes | **Serves:** 4

1 teaspoon olive oil
1½ teaspoons black pepper
¼ teaspoon garlic powder
¼ teaspoon thyme
⅛ teaspoon cayenne pepper
4 (100g) red snapper fillets, skin on
4 thin slices of lemon
Cooking spray

1. Grease the baking pan with cooking spray. 2. Mix up the olive oil, black pepper, garlic powder, thyme, and cayenne pepper in a small bowl. 3. Coat the fillets with the mixture on all sides. 4. Arrange the fillets, skin-side down, to the cooking tray and top each fillet with a slice of lemon. 5. Bake the food at 195°C for 10 minutes. 6. Flip the fillets halfway through. 7. When done, remove the lemon slices and let the fillets cool for 5 minutes before serving.

Per Serving: Calories 97; Fat 6.28g; Sodium 139mg; Carbs 3.76g; Fibre 2.3g; Sugar 0.33g; Protein 6.71g

Fried Catfish Fillets

Prep Time: 15 minutes | **Cook Time:** 10 minutes | **Serves:** 4

1½ teaspoons cajun seasoning
120ml buttermilk
225 – 350g catfish fillets, cut into 5cm strips if the fillets are large
65g plain flour
50g polenta
1 teaspoon salt
½ teaspoon ground black pepper
2 tablespoons vegetable oil
Lemon wedges, for serving
Tartar sauce, for serving

1. Toss the Creole seasoning and buttermilk in a small mixing dish; evenly coat the catfish fillets with the mixture. 2. Combine the flour, polenta, salt, and black pepper in another bowl. 3. Coat the fillets with the polenta mixture and then transfer the fillets to a plate. 4. Drizzle the fillets with vegetable oil and turn to coat evenly. 5. Place the fillets on the cooking tray. 6. Air fry the fillets at 205°C for 10 minutes. 7. When done, serve and enjoy.

Per Serving: Calories 317; Fat 17.16g; Sodium 749mg; Carbs 24.83g; Fibre 1.2g; Sugar 2.12g; Protein 14.66g

Crisp Flounder Fillets

Prep Time: 5 minutes | **Cook Time:** 15 minutes | **Serves:** 4

100g dry breadcrumbs
60ml vegetable oil
4 flounder fillets
1 egg, beaten
1 lemon, sliced

1. In a suitable bowl, mix the breadcrumbs and vegetable oil until the mixture becomes loose and crumbly. 2. Beat the egg in another bowl. 3. Dip the fillets into the egg; shake off any excess. Then dip the fillets into the breadcrumb mixture; coat evenly and thoroughly. 4. Place the fillets on the baking pan. 5. Air fry the fillets at 175°C for 15 minutes. 6. Serve warm after cooking.

Per Serving: Calories 451; Fat 31.43g; Sodium 461mg; Carbs 22.9g; Fibre 7.1g; Sugar 13.44g; Protein 22.03g

Grilled Lobster Tail

Prep Time: 10 minutes | **Cook Time:** 10 minutes | **Serves:** 4

150g of lobster tails, shell cut from the top
⅛ teaspoon salt
⅛ teaspoon black pepper
⅛ teaspoon paprika
1 tablespoon butter
½ lemon, cut into wedges
Chopped parsley for garnish

1. Place the processed lobster tails in the baking pan. 2. In the bowl, mix up the remaining ingredients and then pour over the lobster tails. 3. Grill the lobster tails at 205°C for 8 minutes. 4. Serve warm.

Per Serving: Calories 65; Fat 3.34g; Sodium 289mg; Carbs 1.47g; Fibre 0.6g; Sugar 0.29g; Protein 7.54g

Garlicky Salmon

Prep Time: 10 minutes | **Cook Time:** 10 minutes | **Serves:** 3

2 Salmon Fillets
½ teaspoon lemon pepper
½ teaspoon garlic powder
Salt and pepper to taste
80ml soy sauce
65g sugar
1 tablespoon olive oil

1. Sprinkle the salmon fillets with garlic powder, lemon powder, salt, and pepper. 2. Add 80ml of water to a shallow bowl and combine the olive oil, soy sauce, and sugar; immerse in the salmon fillets sauce. 3. Cover the fillets with cling film and marinate them in the refrigerator for at least 1 hour. 4. Air fry the fillets at 175°C for 10 minutes until they are tender. 5. Serve warm.

Per Serving: Calories 484; Fat 19.55g; Sodium 556mg; Carbs 18.83g; Fibre 0.8g; Sugar 16.18g; Protein 55.34g

Jumbo Lump Crab Cakes

Prep Time: 10 minutes | **Cook Time:** 10 minutes | **Serves:** 4

200g jumbo lump crabmeat
1 tablespoon mixed herbs
35g bread crumbs
35g diced red pepper
35g chopped green pepper
1 egg
60g mayonnaise
Juice of ½ lemon
1 teaspoon flour
Cooking oil

1. In a large mixing bowl, mix the crabmeat, herbs, bread crumbs, red pepper, green pepper, egg, mayonnaise, and lemon juice. 2. Form the mixture into four patties; sprinkle each cake with ¼ teaspoon of flour. 3. Arrange the cakes in the baking pan and then coat them with the cooking oil. 4. Bake the cakes at 180°C for 10 minutes. 5. Serve warm.

Per Serving: Calories 142; Fat 11.24g; Sodium 573mg; Carbs 7.11g; Fibre 1.9g; Sugar 0.9g; Protein 4.18g

Cod Fillets

Prep Time: 10 minutes | **Cook Time:** 12 minutes | **Serves:** 4

4 cod fillets
¼ teaspoon fine sea salt
1 teaspoon cayenne pepper
¼ teaspoon ground black pepper, or more to taste
10g fresh parsley, coarsely chopped
120ml milk
4 garlic cloves, minced
1 pepper, chopped
1 teaspoon dried basil
½ teaspoon dried oregano
Cooking spray

1. Lightly grease a baking pan with cooking spray. 2. Season the fillets with salt, cayenne pepper, and black pepper. 3. Pulse the remaining ingredients in a food processor and transfer the mixture to a bowl. 4. Coat the fillets with the mixture, and then place them in the baking pan. 5. Air fry the fillets at 190°C for 12 minutes. 6. When the fillets are flaky, serve.

Per Serving: Calories 280; Fat 21.31g; Sodium 581mg; Carbs 12.33g; Fibre 1g; Sugar 5.9g; Protein 21.31g

Tuna Cakes

Prep Time: 10 minutes | **Cook Time:** 12 minutes | **Serves:** 4

2 (150g) cans of water-packed plain tuna
2 teaspoons Dijon mustard
50g breadcrumbs
1 tablespoon fresh lime juice
2 tablespoons fresh parsley, chopped
1 egg
3 tablespoons rapeseed oil
Salt and ground black pepper to taste

1. Drain most of the liquid from the canned tuna. 2. Mix the drained tunas with the mustard, crumbs, lemon juice, parsley, and hot sauce till well combined. 3. Add a little rapeseed oil if it seems too dry. Add egg and salt and stir them to combine. 4. Form the patties from the tuna mixture and then let the cakes sit in the refrigerator for about 2 hours. 5. Arrange the patties in the baking pan. 6. Bake the patties at 180°C for 12 minutes. 7. Serve warm.

Per Serving: Calories 223; Fat 14.16g; Sodium 259mg; Carbs 11.62g; Fibre 1g; Sugar 1.68g; Protein 12.7g

Cheese Fillets

Prep Time: 10 minutes | **Cook Time:** 15 minutes | **Serves:** 4

455g salmon or halibut fillet
115g butter
2½ tablespoons mayonnaise
2½ tablespoons lemon juice
75g Parmesan cheese, grated

1. Spritz the fillets with cooking spray. 2. Mix the butter, mayonnaise, and lemon juice in the bowl; stir in the grated Parmesan cheese. 3. Coat the fillets with the mixture and place the fillets on the cooking tray. 4. Roast the fillets at 190°C for 12 minutes. 5. Serve hot.

Per Serving: Calories 488; Fat 39.37g; Sodium 1084mg; Carbs 3.57g; Fibre 0.1g; Sugar 0.35g; Protein 29.56g

Tasty Salmon Fillets

Prep Time: 35 minutes | **Cook Time:** 10 minutes | **Serves:** 4

80g maple syrup
3 tablespoons low-sodium soy sauce
½ teaspoon garlic powder
½ teaspoon coarsely ground black pepper
455g salmon fillets

1. Prepare a large Ziploc bag, add the maple syrup, soy sauce, garlic powder, and pepper, seal the bag and shake to make sure everything gets combined. 2. Open the bag and add the salmon fillets. Place the bag in the fridge and marinate the fillets for 30 minutes. 3. Place the marinated salmon fillets in the baking pan. 4. Roast the fillets at 175°C for 10 minutes. 5. When done, serve.

Per Serving: Calories 249; Fat 8.19g; Sodium 878mg; Carbs 18.51g; Fibre 0.2g; Sugar 15.78g; Protein 24.47g

Fish Pineapple Mix

Prep Time: 20 minutes | **Cook Time:** 15 minutes | **Serves:** 6

250g fish filet, sliced into ½cm thin slices
2 tablespoons corn flour mixed with 2 tablespoons plain flour
80ml cooking oil
4 shallots, peeled and halved
35g green pepper, diced
35g red pepper, diced
35g yellow pepper, diced
1 tomato, cut into wedges
50g canned pineapple, diced
For the sweet and sour sauce:
5 tablespoons tomato sauce
3 tablespoons chili sauce
3 tablespoons plum sauce
1 tablespoon lemon juice
2 tablespoons brown sugar
½ teaspoon salt or to taste

1. Heat all the sauce ingredients in a saucepan over medium-high heat, and bring to a gentle boil. Turn off the heat and set the sauce aside for later use. 2. Coat the fish slices thoroughly in the flour mixture. Shake off the excess and discard. Set aside. 3. Place the fish on the baking pan and sprinkle oil over the top. 4. Roast the fish at 205°C for 10 minutes until the fish is light brown. 5. Add the sauce on top of the fish and toss. If the sauce is too thick, add 2 to 3 tablespoons of water, and the sauce should still be slightly thick and sticky, not watery. 6. Roast the food for 5 minutes longer. 7. Toss the fish once done to coat it in the sauce thoroughly.

Per Serving: Calories 309; Fat 19.86g; Sodium 590mg; Carbs 22.6g; Fibre 2.2g; Sugar 14.75g; Protein 10.34g

Mackerel Fillets

Prep Time: 10 minutes | **Cook Time:** 10 minutes | **Serves:** 4

2 mackerel fillets
2 tablespoons red chili flakes
2 teaspoons garlic, minced
1 teaspoon lemon juice

1. Mix the mackerel fillets with the red chili flakes, minced garlic, and a drizzle of lemon juice. 2. Allow them to sit for 5 minutes. 3. Air fry the fillets at 175°C for 10 minutes. 4. Flip the fillets halfway through cooking. 5. Plate the fillets, making sure to spoon any remaining juice over them before serving.

Per Serving: Calories 211; Fat 3.98g; Sodium 343mg; Carbs 0.82g; Fibre 0g; Sugar 0.05g; Protein 40.3g

Seasoned Prawn

Prep Time: 5 minutes | **Cook Time:** 15 minutes | **Serves:** 2

1 tablespoon olive oil
1 lemon, juiced
1 teaspoon lemon pepper
¼ teaspoon paprika
¼ teaspoon garlic powder
300g uncooked medium prawns, peeled and deveined
1 lemon, sliced

1. Mix the olive oil, lemon juice, lemon pepper, paprika, and garlic powder in a bowl. 2. Coat the prawns with the paprika mixture. 3. Place the coated prawn onto the cooking tray. 4. Air fry the prawn at 175°C for 15 minutes. 5. Let the prawns cool for 5 minutes before serving with the lemon slices.

Per Serving: Calories 202; Fat 8.67g; Sodium 965mg; Carbs 7.44g; Fibre 0.6g; Sugar 2.4g; Protein 23.88g

Polenta Squid

Prep Time: 10 minutes | **Cook Time:** 15 minutes | **Serves:** 6

½ teaspoon salt
½ teaspoon mixed herbs
50g plain polenta
90g semolina flour
1 to 2 pinches of pepper
1.4L olive oil
675g baby squid, rinsed

1. Slice the tentacles of the squid, keeping just ½ cm of the hood in one piece. 2. In the bowl, mix up the herbs, polenta, flours, salt, and 1 to 2 pinches of pepper. 3. Dredge squid pieces into the flour mixture and then arrange them into the cooking tray, liberally spray them with the olive oil. 4. Air fry the food at 175°C for 15 minutes. 5. When the coating turns a golden brown, turn off the air fryer.

Per Serving: Calories 1423; Fat 114.63g; Sodium 458mg; Carbs 93.44g; Fibre 3g; Sugar 48.02g; Protein 8.63g

Fish Fingers

Prep Time: 10 minutes | **Cook Time:** 15 minutes | **Serves:** 2

455g of fish fillets
65g plain flour
1 teaspoon salt, divided
½ teaspoon ground black pepper divided
2 eggs
100g dried breadcrumbs

1. Season the fish fillets with salt and let them marinate for 20 to 30 minutes. 2. In a suitable bowl, mix the flour with salt and pepper; in the second bowl, beat the eggs, and in the third bowl, add the dried breadcrumbs. 3. Dredge the fillets in the flour, dip them in egg and then thoroughly coat them with breadcrumbs. 4. Air fry the fillets at 205°C for 15 minutes. 5. After 10 minutes of cooking time, flip the fillets and then resume cooking them in the air fryer. 6. When done, serve and enjoy.

Per Serving: Calories 658; Fat 26.13g; Sodium 1411mg; Carbs 53.56g; Fibre 4.8g; Sugar 25.41g; Protein 51.29g

Tilapia Tacos with Sauce

Prep Time: 30 minutes | **Cook Time:** 30 minutes | **Serves:** 12

Fish Taco
24 small white corn tortillas
675g tilapia
½ teaspoon ground cumin
½ teaspoon cayenne pepper
1 teaspoon salt
¼ teaspoon black pepper
1 tablespoon olive oil
1 tablespoon butter

Taco Toppings
½ small purple cabbage
2 medium avocados, sliced
½ red onion, diced
½ bunch coriander, longer stems removed
100g feta cheese, grated
1 lime, cut into 8 wedges, to serve

Taco Sauce
120g sour cream
80g mayonnaise
2 tablespoons lime juice from 1 medium lime
1 teaspoon garlic powder
1 teaspoon Sriracha sauce or to taste

1. Line the baking pan with parchment. 2. Add ½ teaspoon of cumin, ½ teaspoon of cayenne pepper, one teaspoon of salt, and ¼ teaspoon of black pepper to a small bowl and mix them well. 3. Evenly sprinkle the seasoning mix over both sides of the tilapia. 4. Arrange the fish on the baking pan, drizzle with olive oil and dot each piece with butter. 5. Bake the fish at 190°C for 25 minutes. 6. To brown the edges, turn the dial to grill and grill the fish for 3 to 5 minutes at the end of the baking time, if desired. 7. Mix all the taco sauce ingredients in a bowl until well blended. 8. In a dry frying pan, quickly toast the corn tortillas over medium-high heat. 9. Arrange the fish pieces on the tortillas, add the remaining ingredients, and finish with a generous sprinkle of feta cheese and the awesome taco sauce!

Per Serving: Calories 254; Fat 13.85g; Sodium 467mg; Carbs 18.72g; Fibre 4.5g; Sugar 2.52g; Protein 16.23g

Crab Meat Prawn Roll

Prep Time: 20 minutes | **Cook Time:** 15 minutes | **Serves:** 12

2 tablespoons butter
80g onion, finely diced
35g red pepper, finely diced
35g green pepper, finely diced
455g crabmeat
55g panko crumbs
12 Ritz crackers, crushed
1 teaspoon lemon zest
½ teaspoon cayenne pepper
½ tsp mixed herbs
120g mayonnaise
1 large egg
Salt and pepper
24 jumbo or large prawns
2 tablespoons butter, melted

1. Melt the butter in a nonstick pan over medium-high heat. 2. Sauté the onion, red pepper, and green pepper with the melted butter for 3 minutes or until soft. Let cool. 3. Pick through the crabmeat and remove any shell. Place the crab in a medium bowl, add the panko crumbs, Ritz crackers, lemon zest, cayenne pepper, mayonnaise, and egg and then gently stir them to mix. 4. Season the mixture with salt and pepper and place in the refrigerator. 5. Peel the prawn, leaving the tails on. Cut through the backside of each prawn, like you would to devein it, but cut more deeply, almost all the way through. Remove and discard the veins. 6. Place the prawn on the baking pan, butterflied side down, pressing to flatten. 7. Shape about one heaping tablespoon of crab mixture into a ball and place on top of a prawn, pressing the tail into the top to secure. Do the same with the remaining mixture and prawns. 8. Drizzle the melted butter over the prawn. 9. Roast the food at 175°C for 15 minutes. 10. Serve when done.

Per Serving: Calories 227; Fat 10.58g; Sodium 279mg; Carbs 19.53g; Fibre 7.5g; Sugar 1.02g; Protein 15.92g

Prawn Stuffed Peppers

Prep Time: 10 minutes | **Cook Time:** 50 minutes | **Serves:** 10

1kg cooked rice
1½ tablespoon olive oil
55g butter
900g of medium-sized prawn (peeled and deveined)
1½ teaspoons cajun seasoning
1 large yellow onion, chopped
1 yellow pepper, chopped
2 cloves garlic, chopped
375g can of diced tomatoes
200g can tomato sauce
250g can cream of mushroom
6 red peppers
240 – 480ml of water
150g shredded cheese
Fresh chopped parsley

1. Boil a pot of water. 2. Cut the whole red peppers in half and remove their ribs and seeds; rinse the peppers and use the paper towel to pat them dry. 3. Add the peppers to the boiling water and wait for 5 minutes to parboil them, then arrange them in a large casserole dish. 4. Mix the prawns with the cajun seasoning. 5. Heat the olive oil and butter in a large pot or frying pan over medium-high heat; add the prawns and sauté them for 3 to 5 minutes until cooked through, then transfer them to a bowl. 6. Still in the pot or frying pan, add a little more oil, the onion, chopped green peppers, garlic, and Creole seasoning, and sauté them for 10 minutes or until the onions are transparent. 7. Lower the heat to medium-low and sauté the diced tomatoes, tomato sauce, and cream of mushroom. 8. Add the prawns back to the pot or frying pan and stir in the cooked rice. 9. When cooked, apportion the prawn-rice mixture between the half peppers. 10. Pour about 120 ml of water into the bottom of a casserole dish and then cover the casserole dish with foil. 11. Air fry the food at 175°C for 25 minutes. 12. Once done, carefully remove the foil and top the mixture with a little shredded cheese and fresh parsley.

Per Serving: Calories 507; Fat 25.42g; Sodium 754mg; Carbs 64.84g; Fibre 20.4g; Sugar 4.94g; Protein 30.89g

Flounder Fillets

Prep Time: 10 minutes | **Cook Time:** 12 minutes | **Serves:** 3

1 egg
100g dry breadcrumbs
60ml vegetable oil
3 (150g) flounder fillets
1 lemon, sliced

1. Crack the egg into a small bowl and beat well. 2. Mix the breadcrumbs and oil in another bowl until a crumbly mixture is formed. 3. Dip flounder fillets into the beaten egg and then coat with the breadcrumb mixture. 4. Arrange the flounder fillets to the baking pan. 5. Air fry the fillets at 175°C for 12 minutes. 6. Serve hot.

Per Serving: Calories 488; Fat 31.71g; Sodium 562mg; Carbs 32.23g; Fibre 5.1g; Sugar 3.14g; Protein 19.75g

Chapter 5 Chicken and Poultry Recipes

Baked Turkey Breast

Prep Time: 20 minutes | **Cook Time:** 90 minutes | **Serves:** 4

3 strips of thick-cut bacon
3 tablespoons softened unsalted butter, at room temperature
1½ tablespoons minced garlic
1 tablespoon sage leaves, freshly chopped
1½ teaspoons rosemary leaves, freshly chopped
1 teaspoon oregano leaves, freshly chopped
1 teaspoon thyme leaves, freshly chopped
2 teaspoons salt, divided
1 teaspoon freshly ground black pepper, divided
1 (2.7kg) whole turkey breast, rinsed and patted dry

1. Line the cooking tray and line with aluminum foil. 2. In a frying pan, cook the bacon to crisp. Then drain with paper towels. Reserve the rendered bacon fat, about 1 tablespoon. 3. Finely chop the cooked bacon and transfer it to a small bowl. 4. Add in sage, oregano, thyme, butter, 1 teaspoon of salt, ½ teaspoon of pepper, and garlic, and mix well with a spoon until a paste has been formed. 5. Loosen the skin on both sides of the turkey breast to separate it from the meat. 6. Separate the herb paste into 2 and spread gently on the turkey breast. 7. And evenly spread the rest half between the skin and breast. 8. Add the rest salt and pepper to the outside of the turkey to season. 9. Then brush the bacon fat over the turkey. 10. Bake the food at 190°C for 1 hour 30 minutes until the meat thermometer reads the centre of the thickest part at 74°C. 11. When cooked, remove the turkey from the air fryer and let it sit for 20 minutes to cool. 12. Cut into your desired-size slices and serve! Enjoy!

Per Serving: Calories 591; Fat 14.35g; Sodium 1572mg; Carbs 1.88g; Fibre 0.5g; Sugar 0.05g; Protein 107.48g

Chicken Pot Pie

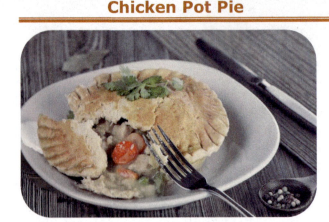

Prep Time: 10 minutes | **Cook Time:** 50 minutes | **Serves:** 8

6 tablespoons butter
150g button mushrooms, chopped
220g onions, chopped
150g carrots, chopped
90g celery, chopped
1 tablespoon garlic, chopped
1 teaspoon salt
1 teaspoon freshly ground black pepper
6 tablespoons flour, plus more for dusting
900g boneless and skinless chicken thigh, cut into bite-size pieces
720ml chicken stock
70g frozen green peas
4 ½ teaspoons parsley, chopped
1 sheet puff pastry, thawed
1 egg, whisked

1. In a suitable saucepan, melt the butter over medium heat. 2. Sauté the onions, celery, carrots, garlic, and mushrooms for 3 minutes. 3. Add the black pepper, salt, and 6 tablespoons of flour to cook together, stirring often. 4. Then add the chicken and cook for about 5 minutes. 5. Pour stock and cook for about 20 minutes, stirring constantly. 6. Turn off the heat. Add parsley and peas and stir well. 7. On a work surface, dust the flour and make the puff pastry over. 8. Invert a suitable casserole dish over the puff pastry and cut around the dish 2.5cm wider than the dish. 9. Pour the veggie mixture into the casserole dish. Cut a small hole in the centre of the pie to vent. 10. Add the egg and 1 tablespoon of water together in a separate dish and whisk together to form an egg wash. Pour the egg wash over the puff pastry. 11. Arrange the casserole dish on the baking pan. 12. Air fry the dish at 205°C for 20 minutes. 13. When cooked, remove from the air fryer carefully. 14. Serve and enjoy!

Per Serving: Calories 311; Fat 14.83g; Sodium 812mg; Carbs 14.16g; Fibre 2g; Sugar 3.3g; Protein 29.53g

Whole Cooked Chicken

Prep Time: 5 minutes | **Cook Time:** 40 minutes | **Serves:** 4

1 (1.6kg) chicken
1 teaspoon salt
1½ teaspoons freshly ground white pepper
1 tablespoon plus 1 teaspoon olive oil
2 tablespoons unsalted butter, room temperature
1 teaspoon garlic, minced
1 teaspoon fresh thyme leaves

1. Rub salt and pepper over the chicken evenly. 2. Prepare the Rotisserie. Remove the forks from the Rotisserie Spit. Insert the Rotisserie Spit into the centre of the chicken. 3. Use the twine to tie the chicken, and then set the rotisserie spit with the chicken inside the air fryer. 4. Cook the chicken at 170°C for 40 minutes on Rotisserie mode. 5. In a small bowl, combine together butter, thyme, and garlic until well whisked. 6. When cooked, remove from the air fryer at once. Drizzle over the chicken with the garlic-butter mixture. 7. Serve and enjoy!

Per Serving: Calories 251; Fat 9.96g; Sodium 721mg; Carbs 0.84g; Fibre 0.3g; Sugar 0.01g; Protein 37.56g

Crusted Chicken Thighs

Prep Time: 10 minutes | **Cook Time:** 40 minutes | **Serves:** 6

480ml buttermilk
2 tablespoons salt
1 teaspoon sugar
½ teaspoon ground black pepper
6 chicken legs
6 chicken thighs
125g flour
6 eggs
250g flaked corn cereal, crushed

1. Add salt, black pepper, buttermilk, and sugar and mix together. Then add the chicken thighs and legs to soak. 2. Whisk the eggs in a shallow baking dish. 3. In a second dish, add the flour. 4. Prepare a third dish with flaked corn cereal. 5. Drain the chicken thighs and legs and get rid of any excess buttermilk. 6. Then dredge the chicken pieces into the flour to coat. Add in the egg mixture. Finally, put the chicken pieces in the corn cereal, pressing them to coat well. 7. Arrange the chicken legs and chicken thighs onto the cooking tray. 8. Bake the fries at 190°C for 40 minutes. 9. Serve and enjoy!

Per Serving: Calories 1524; Fat 56.22g; Sodium 3012mg; Carbs 144.42g; Fibre 12.7g; Sugar 5.6g; Protein 108.7g

Rustic Whole Chicken

Prep Time: 5 minutes | **Cook Time:** 55 minutes | **Serves:** 6

20g Rustic Rub
1.8kg whole chicken, rinsed

1. Toss together the chicken with the Rustic Rub and coat well. 2. Tie the chicken. Force the spit through the centre of the chicken lengthwise, and then slide the forks onto each side of the spit. Tighten the screws to secure them. 3. Transfer the chicken to the air fryer. 4. Cook the chicken at 175°C for 55 minutes on Rotisserie mode. 5. When cooked, the meat thermometer should read 75°C. 6. Allow the chicken to sit for about 15 minutes after cooking. 7. Serve and enjoy!

Per Serving: Calories 339; Fat 8.18g; Sodium 303mg; Carbs 0.73; Fibre 0.2g; Sugar 0.43g; Protein 61.64g

Cream Chicken Parmigiana

Prep Time: 10 minutes | **Cook Time:** 55 minutes | **Serves:** 4

50g Seasoned bread crumbs
25g Grated Parmesan cheese
3 tablespoons Spaghetti sauce mix
1½ teaspoons Garlic powder
4 boneless skinless chicken breast halves
120ml Italian salad dressing
120g Meatless spaghetti sauce
30g Shredded part-skim Mozzarella cheese

1. Combine the bread crumbs, spaghetti sauce mix, garlic powder, and the grated parmesan cheese in a shallow dish. 2. Toss the chicken breast halves with the Italian salad dressing. Add in the breadcrumb mixture and coat well. 3. Grease a baking pan with cooking spray and place the chicken. 4. Bake the chicken breast halves at 175°C for 40 to 45 minutes. 5. Drizzle the meat with Meatless spaghetti sauces and sprinkle the Mozzarella cheese over. Bake for 5 to 7 minutes longer. 6. Serve and enjoy!

Per Serving: Calories 588; Fat 21.22g; Sodium 1324mg; Carbs 26.63g; Fibre 0.9g; Sugar 6.56g; Protein 68.09g

Peanut Butter Chicken Thighs

Prep Time: 15 minutes | **Cook Time:** 22 minutes | **Serves:** 4

455g bone-in skin-on chicken thighs
65g creamy peanut butter
1 tablespoon sriracha sauce
1 tablespoon soy sauce
2 tablespoons Thai sweet chili sauce
2 tablespoons lime juice
1 teaspoon minced garlic
1 teaspoon minced ginger
½ teaspoon salt
120ml hot water

1. Add lime juice, soy sauce, sriracha, salt, sweet chili sauce, and peanut butter to a large bowl and mix well. 2. Stir in hot water until well mixed. 3. In a zip-top bag, add half the sauce and chicken. Shake to mix evenly, and then place in the refrigerator to marinate. 4. Remove from the refrigerator and take the chicken out from the bag. 5. Arrange the chicken onto the cooking tray. 6. Air fry the chicken at 175°C for 20 to 22 minutes. 7. When cooked, remove from the air fryer carefully. 8. Serve and enjoy!

Per Serving: Calories 373; Fat 28.27g; Sodium 646mg; Carbs 6.94g; Fibre 1.7g; Sugar 2.49g; Protein 23.3g

Crunchy Chicken Strips

Prep Time: 10 minutes | **Cook Time:** 10 minutes | **Serves:** 4

65g plain flour
220g panko bread crumbs
2 tablespoons rapeseed oil
1 egg
3 chicken breasts, each cut into four strips, boneless and skinless
Salt and ground black pepper, to taste
Cooking spray

1. Spritz the cooking tray with cooking spray. 2. In a large bowl, add the flour. 3. In a shallow dish, add the rapeseed oil and panko and mix well to combine. 4. In a separate bowl, whisk the egg. 5. Sprinkle salt and pepper over the chicken strips to season. Then dredge in the flour. Shake off any excess. 6. Drop in the egg mixture and coat with the breadcrumbs. 7. Transfer the strips onto the cooking tray. 8. Air fry the chicken strips at 180°C for 10 minutes until the strips are crunchy and lightly browned, flipping the chicken strips halfway through cooking. 9. Serve and enjoy!

Per Serving: Calories 576; Fat 30.29g; Sodium 249mg; Carbs 21.89g; Fibre 1.1g; Sugar 1.77g; Protein 50.98g

Savory Chicken Breasts

Prep Time: 10 minutes | **Cook Time:** 10 minutes | **Serves:** 4

4 (100g) boneless, skinless chicken breasts
Chicken seasoning or rub to taste
Salt and ground black pepper to taste
85g honey
2 tablespoons soy sauce
2 teaspoons grated fresh ginger
2 garlic cloves, minced
Cooking spray

1. Spritz the cooking tray with cooking spray. 2. Sprinkle chicken seasoning, salt, and chicken breast. 3. Transfer the seasoned chicken onto the prepared cooking tray and spritz the chicken with cooking spray. 4. Air fry the chicken breasts at 205°C for 10 minutes, flipping them once halfway through. 5. When cooked, the meat thermometer should read around 75°C. 6. In a large saucepan, heat soy sauce, ginger, garlic, and honey over medium-high heat until thickened, for about 3 minutes. Stir them often. 7. When cooked, carefully remove the chicken from the air fryer and serve with the honey mixture.

Per Serving: Calories 144; Fat 3.09g; Sodium 198mg; Carbs 27.11g; Fibre 0.8g; Sugar 21.07g; Protein 3.6g

Veggies & Chicken Breasts

Prep Time: 10 minutes | **Cook Time:** 15 minutes | **Serves:** 4

225g boneless and skinless chicken breasts
1 large pepper, cut into strips
1 medium red onion, cut into strips
1 tablespoon rapeseed oil
1 tablespoon chili powder
2 teaspoons lime juice
1 teaspoon cumin
Salt and pepper to taste

1. Add pepper, chicken stripes, chili powder, cumin, pepper, onion, rapeseed oil, and salt in a bowl and whisk well. 2. Place the fajitas on the cooking tray. 3. Air fry the food at 190°C for 10 to 13 minutes. 4. Toss them halfway through cooking. 5. Serve and enjoy!

Per Serving: Calories 123; Fat 5.44g; Sodium 86mg; Carbs 5.09g; Fibre 1.4g; Sugar 1.94g; Protein 13.66g

Chicken Wings with Teriyaki Sauce

Prep Time: 10 minutes | **Cook Time:** 25 minutes | **Serves:** 4

900g of chicken wings
120g Teriyaki sauce
2 teaspoons minced garlic
¼ teaspoon ground ginger
2 teaspoons baking powder

1. In a bowl, add the chicken wings, Teriyaki sauce, minced garlic, and ground ginger and combine well. 2. Let the chicken wings marinate in the refrigerator for an hour. 3. Arrange the chicken wings onto the cooking tray and rub the chicken wings with baking powder. 4. Air fry the chicken wings at 205°C for 25 minutes, flipping them several times during cooking. 5. Serve and enjoy!

Per Serving: Calories 323; Fat 8.06g; Sodium 826mg; Carbs 7.33g; Fibre 0.1g; Sugar 5.09g; Protein 52.07g

Spiced Chicken in Egg Mixture

Prep Time: 3 hours 30 minutes | **Cook Time:** 20 minutes | **Serves:** 8

Brine

1.9L buttermilk
4 cloves garlic, crushed
½ white onion, sliced
120ml hot sauce
3 tablespoons salt, to taste
1.3kg fresh whole chicken, cut up

Seasoning blend

1 tablespoon granulated sugar
1 tablespoon salt, as you like
1 tablespoon black pepper
1 tablespoon onion powder
1 tablespoon cayenne plus extra for flavoring
1 tablespoon Cajun seasoning
1 teaspoon celery salt

1 tablespoon paprika
1 tablespoon garlic powder
1 tablespoon poultry seasoning
1 teaspoon smoked salt
½ tablespoon chili powder
375g self-rising flour

Egg mixture

3 eggs
60ml water
120ml hot sauce, plus more as desired
1 teaspoon garlic powder
Peanut oil or shortening for frying
Cajun seasoning for sprinkling

1. Line a roasting bag over a large bowl. Add garlic, onion slices, buttermilk, salt, and 120ml of hot sauce. 2. Tie the bag and soak in the chicken. Place in the refrigerator for up to 3 hours. 3. Drain the chicken and transfer the chicken onto a baking tray. 4. Mix together the seasoning blend and taste to adjust as you like. 5. Then sprinkle evenly over the chicken with up to half the seasoning blend. Set it aside. 6. Combine the flour with the remaining spices and add to a large paper bag. 7. Add the chicken to the bag. Close tightly and shake until coated well. 8. Take the chicken out from the bag and shake off any excess flour. 9. Add water, hot sauce, garlic powder, and the beaten eggs to a large bowl and mix well. 10. Dip the chicken pieces with the egg mixture and get rid of any excess mixture. 11. In the bag again, add the chicken and shake to coat well. 12. Then return the coated chicken to the cooking tray. 13. Air fry the chicken at 205°C for 20 minutes. 14. Serve the dish on a serving plate and sprinkle over with Cajun seasoning immediately.

Per Serving: Calories 447; Fat 9.37g; Sodium 5378mg; Carbs 43.64g; Fibre 2.7g; Sugar 3.91g; Protein 44.35g

Chicken Thighs with Sesame Seeds

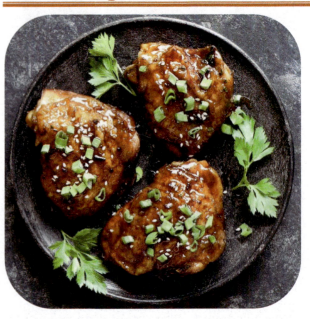

Prep Time: 35 minutes | **Cook Time:** 15 minutes | **Serves:** 4

2 tablespoons sesame oil
2 tablespoons soy sauce
1 tablespoon honey
1 tablespoon sriracha sauce
1 teaspoon rice vinegar
900g of chicken thighs
1 green onion, chopped
2 tablespoons toasted sesame seeds

1. In a large bowl, add soy sauce, sriracha, vinegar, honey, and sesame oil and combine well. 2. Transfer the mixture into an airtight container and place it in the refrigerator for at least 30 minutes. 3. Arrange the food onto the baking pan. 4. Roast the food at 175°C for 15 minutes. 5. When cooked, carefully remove the chicken from the air fryer and transfer it to a plate. Set it aside to cool for 5 minutes. 6. Add sesame seeds and chopped green onion to garnish. 7. Serve and enjoy!

Per Serving: Calories 629; Fat 47.92g; Sodium 362mg; Carbs 9.25g; Fibre 1.2g; Sugar 6.74g; Protein 38.97g

Hot Fried Chicken

Prep Time: 20 minutes | **Cook Time:** 35 minutes | **Serves:** 6

1 L buttermilk
60ml hot sauce
3 tablespoon garlic, minced
2 teaspoons celery salt
2⅓ teaspoons salt, divided
2⅓ teaspoons black pepper, divided
1 (1.8kg) chicken, cut into 8 pieces
4 eggs
120ml milk
500g flour
Pepper Jelly Drizzle
75g seeded red pepper, minced
1 tablespoon crushed red pepper
180ml cider vinegar
650g sugar
2 jalapeño peppers, thinly sliced
2 Fresno chilies, thinly sliced
1 clove of garlic, minced
1 pinch salt

1. Add spicy sauce, celery salt, 2 teaspoons of salt, 1 teaspoon of black pepper, and the buttermilk in a large mixing bowl and mix well. 2. Add the chicken to the mixture and toss to coat well. Place the chicken together with the mixture in the refrigerator and marinate overnight. 3. Then remove the chicken from the refrigerator and set it aside to room temperature, about 1 hour. 4. Drain the chicken from excess marinade. 5. Beat eggs and pour milk into a shallow bowl. In a separate dish, add flour and the remaining salt and pepper and combine well. 6. Dip the chicken pieces in the flour. Coat well and then shake off any excess flour. Then soak in the egg mixture and dip again in the flour. 7. Grease the cooking tray with cooking spray. Arrange the coated chicken pieces evenly onto the cooking tray. 8. Air fry the chicken pieces at 205°C for 35 minutes until the internal temperature of the meat is 74°C. 9. Add crushed red pepper, peppers, and vinegar to a food processor or blender and pulse several times. 10. In a medium heavy saucepan, add the rest Pepper Jelly Drizzle and combine well. 11. Heat the saucepan over high heat on the stovetop and stir them often to boil vigorously. 12. Then remove and let it sit to cool to room temperature. Serve or store the pepper jelly drizzle in an airtight container in your refrigerator for up to 6 months. 13. Drizzle the pepper jelly over the chicken and serve!

Per Serving: Calories 858; Fat 13.25g; Sodium 1683mg; Carbs 131.74g; Fibre 3g; Sugar 63.82g; Protein 49.82g

Curry Chicken Wings

Prep Time: 4 hours | **Cook Time:** 40 minutes | **Serves:** 4

1kg chicken wings, separated at the joints and wing tips discarded
¾ teaspoon salt
2 teaspoons sugar
1 tablespoon Madras curry powder
1 tablespoon fish sauce
2 tablespoons rapeseed oil
1 large shallot, minced
2 Thai chilies, minced (with seeds)
2 stalks of lemongrass, inner bulb chopped finely
1 teaspoon garlic, minced
2 tablespoons fresh coriander, chopped, for garnish

1. Combine chicken wings, salt, sugar, curry powder, fish sauce, oil, shallot, Thai chilies, lemongrass, and garlic in a large re-sealable plastic bag. 2. Seal the bag and distribute the spices evenly around the chicken. Then place in the refrigerator and marinate for at least 4 hours or overnight. 3. Allow the chicken to sit at room temperature. 4. On the cooking tray, add the marinated chicken. 5. Air fry the chicken wings at 205°C for 40 minutes until the internal temperature reaches 74°C, flipping the chicken every 10 minutes to ensure the chicken is evenly cooked. 6. Set the chicken aside to cool. Serve warm!

Per Serving: Calories 418; Fat 16.65g; Sodium 1051mg; Carbs 6.6g; Fibre 1.4g; Sugar 1.73g; Protein 58.5g

Herbed Turkey Roast

Prep Time: 15 minutes | **Cook Time:** 2 hours 30 minutes | **Serves:** 12

1(5.4 – 6.3kg) whole turkey, thawed if frozen
3 tablespoons extra-virgin olive oil
1 teaspoon salt
½ teaspoon freshly ground black pepper
3 sprigs of fresh rosemary
2 sprigs of fresh thyme
2 sprigs of fresh sage
2 sprigs of fresh oregano
1 lemon, halved
2 carrots, halved
4 celery stalks, halved
960ml chicken stock
960ml water

Cranberry Gravy

220g sweetened dried cranberries
240ml water
50g sugar
2 teaspoons fresh sage leaves, chopped
90g plain flour
185g butter
960ml chicken stock

1. Rinse both inside and out of the turkey and brush it with oil. 2. Add salt and pepper to season, pressing to coat. 3. Fill in the cavity of the turkey with 2 rosemary sprigs, lemon halves, 1 oregano sprig, 1 sage sprig, and 1 oregano sprig. 4. Place the turkey onto the baking pan. 5. Arrange celery, carrots, and the rest herbs on the bottom of the pan around the turkey. Pour 960 ml of stock and 960 ml water over the herbs and vegetables. 6. Roast them at 170°C for 2 hours 30 minutes, basting the stock over the chicken every 30 minutes. 7. When the chicken is cooked, the internal temperature should be 74°C. 8. Carefully remove it from the air fryer and let it cool for 15 minutes. Reserve the chicken stock mixture and discard the vegetables. 9. Add 240ml of water, sugar, and cranberries to a suitable saucepan. Simmer until the cranberries are tender, about 20 minutes. 10. Then let it cool for about 5 minutes. 11. Add 2 teaspoons of sage and the cranberry mixture to a blender and blend until smooth. Set it aside for later use. 12. Add the flour and butter to a medium and heavy saucepan. Cook them +over medium heat for about 3 to 4 minutes and stir it often until a roux has been formed. Then add 960ml of stock, the cranberry puree, and the reserved stock. Bring to a boil over high heat. 13. Simmer and stir to thicken the sauce. 14. Enjoy!

Per Serving: Calories 208; Fat 14.22g; Sodium 963mg; Carbs 16.08g; Fibre 0.7g; Sugar 8.45g; Protein 4.56g

Herb Chicken Thighs

Prep Time: 20 minutes | **Cook Time:** 50 minutes | **Serves:** 8

1.3kg of bone-in chicken thighs
2 tablespoons avocado oil
60ml fresh lemon juice
1 teaspoon lemon zest
1½ tablespoons fresh rosemary, chopped
2 teaspoon ground ginger
1 teaspoon paprika
½ teaspoon sea salt, to taste
1 whole lemon, sliced

1. Prepare a large zip-lock bag, add the chicken thighs, avocado oil, lemon zest, chopped fresh rosemary, ground ginger, sea salt, and lemon juice, and then seal the bag. 2. Place in the refrigerator to marinate for at least 20 minutes and up to 12 hours. 3. In a large cast-iron frying pan, coat inside the frying pan with a single layer of oil and heat over high heat. 4. Once the oil is heated, sear the chicken skin-side down for 3 to 5 minutes until crispy and golden brown. Flip and sear for 3 to 5 minutes. 5. Carefully transfer the chicken to a serving plate and repeat the cooking steps for the rest chicken. 6. In a frying pan, add all the crispy chicken and its juices. Add the lemon slices to the chicken. Cover the chicken with foil. 7. Bake the food in the air fryer at 175°C for 40 minutes. 8. When cooked, carefully remove and serve.

Per Serving: Calories 413; Fat 31.86g; Sodium 284mg; Carbs 1.95g; Fibre 0.3g; Sugar 0.4g; Protein 28.24g

Homemade Popcorn Chicken

Prep Time: 30 Minutes
Cook Time: 6 Minutes

Prep Time: 30 minutes | **Cook Time:** 10 minutes | **Serves:** 4

675g boneless, skinless chicken thighs
Marinade
1 medium head of garlic
1cm ginger, peeled and minced
3 green onions, minced
2 tablespoons soy sauce
1 tablespoon mirin
1 teaspoon cornflour
½ teaspoon five-spice
½ teaspoon ground white pepper
¼ teaspoon ground Sichuan peppercorns
Coating
1 medium egg
120ml cold water
255 – 300g cornflour
Salt, white pepper, and five-spice, to taste

1. Cut the chicken into 2.5cm chunks. 2. In a large bowl, add the chicken chunks. 3. Mince the garlic. 4. In a small bowl, add the minced garlic, ginger, minced green onions, cornflour, mirin, white pepper, five-spice, and pepper, and mix well to make the marinade. 5. Then sprinkle onto the chicken chunks and mix together to coat. Place the chicken in the refrigerator for at least half an hour or overnight. 6. In a medium-sized bowl, beat the eggs with 120ml of water with a fork. 7. Add the cornflour to a separate medium bowl. 8. Dip the chicken in the egg mixture with tongs or chopsticks, and then in the cornflour. 9. Air fry the chicken chunks at 170°C for 3 to 4 minutes until golden brown. 10. Do the same with the remaining chicken pieces. 11. Once the chicken pieces are cooked, transfer to a serving bowl and sprinkle with enough salt, pepper, and a little bit five-spice. 12. Serve and enjoy!

Per Serving: Calories 382; Fat 12.41g; Sodium 596mg; Carbs 48.25g; Fibre 5.4g; Sugar 14.53g; Protein 19.36g

Veggies Chicken Pie

Prep Time: 20 minutes | **Cook Time:** 30 minutes | **Serves:** 8

4 tablespoons unsalted butter
455g boneless skinless chicken breast, cut into small bite-size pieces
130g sliced carrots
60g sliced celery
80g chopped yellow onion
1¼ teaspoons salt
½ teaspoon garlic powder
½ teaspoon dried thyme leaves
¼ teaspoon ground black pepper
30g plain flour
120g heavy cream
240ml chicken stock
70g frozen peas
2 tablespoons freshly minced flat-leaf parsley
2 unbaked pie crusts, 1 top and 1 bottom

1. Add the butter to a large frying pan, and heat it over medium heat. Once the butter is just about to bubble, add the carrots, salt, celery, garlic powder, pepper, thyme leaves, chicken, and onion. Cook in the frying pan for about 8 to 10 minutes, stirring them often. 2. Stir in flour and make sure no flour remains. Then add cream and then the chicken stock. Stir and cook for 3 to 4 minutes, or until the cooking liquid is thick and bubbling. 3. Remove it from heat and add the parsley and peas. Stir well and allow it to cool for the pie fillings, about 3 to 4 minutes. 4. In a 23cm pie plate, add 1 pie crust and then fill in the pie filling. Add the second pie crust. Then seal the edges of the pie crust together and cut 3 to 4 slits in the top crust as a vent. 5. Transfer the plate onto an oven-safe baking pan. 6. Bake the pie at 170°C for 30 minutes. 7. When cooked, remove from the air fryer. Allow it to cool for about 15 to 30 minutes. 8. Slice and serve!

Per Serving: Calories 405; Fat 23.03g; Sodium 817mg; Carbs 25.26g; Fibre 1.4g; Sugar 0.65g; Protein 23.16g

Marinated Turkey Thighs

Prep Time: 60 minutes | **Cook Time:** 35 minutes | **Serves:** 4

240ml buttermilk
160g maple syrup
1 egg
1 teaspoon granulated garlic
4 skin-on, bone-in turkey thighs
Dry mix:
85g plain flour
1 tablespoon salt
1 teaspoon sweet paprika
½ teaspoon smoked paprika
1 teaspoon granulated onion
¼ teaspoon ground black pepper
¼ teaspoon cayenne pepper
½ teaspoon granulated garlic
½ teaspoon honey powder

1. In a re-sealable bag, add the maple syrup, buttermilk, 1 teaspoon granulated garlic, and egg, and combine well. Then add the chicken thighs and seal. Put the sealed bag in the refrigerator and let it marinate for at least 1 hour or up to overnight. 2. Add tapioca flour, sweet paprika, flour, granulated onion, pepper, cayenne pepper, honey powder, ½ teaspoon granulated garlic, salt, smoked paprika, and salt in a shallow dish. 3. Remove the marinated chicken from the bag and drain excess sauce. Add the chicken to the flour mixture and coat well. Shake off any excess. 4. Prepare the cooking tray and spray with cooking spray. 5. Air fry the turkey thighs at 205°C for 35 minutes until the internal temperature reaches 74°C. 6. When cooked, remove from the air fryer carefully. Serve and enjoy!

Per Serving: Calories 784; Fat 53.5g; Sodium 1957mg; Carbs 58.96g; Fibre 1.7g; Sugar 32.39g; Protein 17.71g

Turkey Breast and Bacon

Prep Time: 10 minutes | **Cook Time:** 40 minutes | **Serves:** 4

3 strips of thick-cut bacon
1½ tablespoons garlic, minced
1 tablespoon fresh sage, chopped
1½ teaspoons fresh rosemary, chopped
1 teaspoon fresh oregano, chopped
1 teaspoon fresh thyme, chopped
3 tablespoons unsalted butter, softened
2 teaspoons salt, divided
1 teaspoon freshly ground black pepper, divided
1 (1.1 – 1.3kg) half-turkey breast, rinsed & patted dry

1. Add the bacon to a frying pan and cook over medium-high heat until crisp. Reserve 1 tablespoon of bacon fat and then drain the bacon with a paper towel. 2. Finely cut the bacon and transfer it to a small bowl. 3. Mix in the sage, oregano, butter, thyme, 1 teaspoon salt, rosemary, garlic, and ½ teaspoon black pepper and stir to make a paste. 4. Separate the skin from the flesh by loosening the skin gently on the turkey breast with fingertips. 5. Rub the remaining salt and black pepper over the outside of the chicken breast to season and brush over with the reserved bacon fat. 6. Arrange the seasoned chicken breast on the cooking tray. 7. Bake the food at 165°C for 30 minutes until the internal temperature reads 75°C. 8. When cooked, remove the turkey from the air fryer carefully. Set it aside to cool for about 20 minutes. 9. Cut the turkey into thin slices. 10. Serve with your favored dipping. Enjoy!

Per Serving: Calories 216; Fat 13.43g; Sodium 1276mg; Carbs 2.24g; Fibre 0.7g; Sugar 0.05g; Protein 21.08g

Spiced Turkey Breast

Prep Time: 30 minutes | **Cook Time:** 2 hours | **Serves:** 6

1 whole bone-in turkey breast
3 garlic cloves, finely chopped
1 tablespoon fresh rosemary leaves, chopped
1 tablespoon fresh thyme leaves, chopped
1 tablespoon fresh sage leaves, chopped
2 teaspoons salt
½ teaspoon freshly ground black pepper
2 tablespoons extra-virgin olive oil
2 teaspoons Dijon mustard
120ml freshly squeezed orange juice
2 tablespoons freshly squeezed lemon juice
120ml chicken stock
1 orange, sliced

1. In a heavy baking pan, add the turkey breast, skin-side up. 2. Add the rosemary, sage, thyme, salt, garlic, olive oil, mustard, and pepper and combine well to make a paste. 3. Lift the skin away from the breast. Then spread half of the paste on the meat. Rub the remaining paste all over the outside of the turkey. 4. Add lemon juice, chicken stock, and orange juice into the baking pan. Spread over the pan with orange slices. 5. Roast the breast at 165°C for 2 hours until the chicken is cooked with its skin golden brown. 6. Transfer to a serving bowl and part-skim the fat on top of the juice.

Per Serving: Calories 389; Fat 7.14g; Sodium 1140mg; Carbs 5.4g; Fibre 0.5g; Sugar 3.18g; Protein 71.6g

Panko Chicken Wings

Prep Time: 10 minutes | **Cook Time:** 18 minutes | **Serves:** 4

900g of chicken wings
Cooking spray
Marinade:
240ml buttermilk
½ teaspoon salt
½ teaspoon black pepper
Coating:
125g flour
110g panko bread crumbs
2 tablespoons poultry seasoning
2 teaspoons salt

1. Add salt, buttermilk, and black pepper, and whisk well to marinate the chicken. 2. Add the chicken wings to the marinade bowl and toss to coat well. Set it aside to marinate for at least 1 hour. 3. Prepare the cooking tray and spritz with cooking spray. 4. In a shallow bowl, add the flour, panko bread crumbs, poultry seasoning, and salt together and combine well. 5. Transfer the marinated chicken to toss in the bread crumb mixture and coat well. 6. Air fry the meat at 180°C for 18 minutes, flipping them once halfway through. 7. When cooked, remove from the air fryer and transfer to a serving plate. 8. Serve and enjoy!

Per Serving: Calories 455; Fat 9.34g; Sodium 1798mg; Carbs 32.79g; Fibre 1.4g; Sugar 3.56g; Protein 56.11g

Chapter 6 Beef, Pork, and Lamb Recipes

Steak with Chimichurri Sauce

Prep Time: 2 hours | **Cook Time:** 20 minutes | **Serves:** 4

240ml extra virgin olive oil
160ml sherry wine vinegar
2 tablespoons lime juice
30g coriander, chopped
5g fresh basil leaves, chopped
1 tablespoon fresh marjoram leaves, chopped
3 tablespoons garlic, minced
2 tablespoons shallots, minced
¼ teaspoon crushed red pepper
2½ teaspoons salt, divided
¾ teaspoon fresh cracked black pepper, divided
1 (800 – 900g) flank steak

1. Add olive oil, lime juice, basil, garlic, shallots, sherry vinegar, coriander, and marjoram in a food processor and pulse until it is just fully combined. 2. Add ½ teaspoon salt, ¼ teaspoon black pepper, and crushed red pepper to a mixing bowl and mix to make the chimichurri sauce. 3. Reserve 1 cup of the chimichurri sauce in a non-reactive bowl. Cover with plastic wrap and let it stand for up to 6 hours at room temperature or in the refrigerator overnight. 4. Add 1 teaspoon salt and ¼ teaspoon black pepper to season the steak. Add the steak to a large resealable plastic bag. 5. Add the remaining chimichurri sauce to the bag. Seal the bag and place it in the refrigerator for at least 2 hours. 6. Brush off the excess sauce from the steak and place it on the cooking tray. 7. Air fry the food at 205°C for 18 minutes. 8. Transfer the meat to a clean cutting board. Allow it to rest for 5 to 7 minutes. 9. Slice across the grain into thin strips. 10. Serve and enjoy!

Per Serving: Calories 296; Fat 25.47g; Sodium 1946mg; Carbs 4.73g; Fibre 0.8g; Sugar 0.81g; Protein 10.24g

Beef and Broccoli Florets

Prep Time: 5 minutes | **Cook Time:** 15 minutes | **Serves:** 8

120ml low-sodium soy sauce
4 to 5 cloves garlic, finely minced
2 to 3 tablespoons of honey
2 tablespoons packed brown sugar
2 tablespoons sesame oil
2 tablespoons rice vinegar
2 to 3 teaspoons of ground ginger
1 teaspoon salt
1 teaspoon freshly ground black pepper, or to taste
455g flank steak, sliced against the grain in bite-size pieces
350g of broccoli florets
1 tablespoon cornflour (optional)
1 tablespoon cold water (optional)
2 to 3 green onions, sliced in 2.5cm segments on the bias (optional for garnishing)
1 tablespoon sesame seeds (optional for garnishing)

1. Line a sheet pan with aluminum foil. 2. In a large bowl, add garlic, soy sauce, honey, sesame oil, rice vinegar, salt, pepper, ginger, brown sugar, and any optional red pepper flakes or cayenne, and whisk well. 3. Add the steak and stir well. Marinate for 10 to 15 minutes. 4. Evenly arrange the marinated steak onto the baking pan. Set aside for later use. 5. Dunk the broccoli in the marinade mixture. Transfer the broccoli to the baking pan with a slotted spoon. Place the broccoli between the steak. Reserve the marinade. 6. Roast the food at 220°C for 12 minutes until the broccoli is just tender and the steak is completely cooked. 7. Carefully remove from the air fryer and transfer to a serving plate. 8. Drizzle with the reserved sauce as you desire. 9. Serve and enjoy!

Per Serving: Calories 150; Fat 6.42g; Sodium 902mg; Carbs 8.82g; Fibre 0.8g; Sugar 6.47g; Protein 14.41g

Honey-Glazed Pork Chops

Prep Time: 5 minutes | **Cook Time:** 25 minutes | **Serves:** 4

2 tablespoons honey
4 cloves garlic, minced
2 tablespoons low sodium soy sauce
1 tablespoon no-salt ketchup
½ tablespoon sweet chili sauce
½ teaspoon dried oregano
4 (100g each) bone-in pork chops, fat trimmed
2 tablespoons olive oil
1 tablespoon butter
Fresh parsley, chopped, for garnish

1. Add garlic, honey, soy sauce, chili sauce, ketchup, and oregano in a small mixing bowl and mix well. 2. In a large bowl, add the pork chops and the sauce mixture. Mix well. 3. In an oven-safe 15 cm frying pan, add olive oil and heat over medium-high heat. 4. Then add the pork and sauce to the heated frying pan and sear for about 4 minutes or more, until both sides are just browned. 5. Turn off the heat. Add butter and the pork chops to the cooking tray. 6. Air fry the pork chops at 205°C for 18 minutes. 7. The internal meat thermometer should read 70°C. 8. Carefully remove the tray from the air fryer. 9. Add fresh parsley for garnishment. 10. Serve and enjoy!

Per Serving: Calories 457; Fat 27.05g; Sodium 394mg; Carbs 10.65g; Fibre 0.4g; Sugar 8.94g; Protein 41.19g

Rosemary Lamb Roast

Prep Time: 5 minutes | **Cook Time:** 15 minutes | **Serves:** 2

250g lamb leg roast
1 tablespoon olive oil
1 teaspoon rosemary, fresh or dried
1 teaspoon thyme, fresh or dried
½ teaspoon black pepper

1. Add thyme, rosemary, and olive oil to a plate and mix well. 2. Pat the lamb roast dry. Coat it with the herb-oil mixture. 3. Place the coated lamb onto the cooking tray. 4. Air fry the lamb at 180°C for 15 minutes. 5. When the cooking time is up, carefully remove it from the air fryer, cover it with kitchen foil, and let it stand to cool for about 5 minutes. 6. Serve and enjoy!

Per Serving: Calories 320; Fat 17.11g; Sodium 98mg; Carbs 0.65g; Fibre 0.3g; Sugar 0g; Protein 38.64g

Braised Steak

Prep Time: 10 minutes | **Cook Time:** 8 hours | **Serves:** 8

8 pieces of cubed steak
1¾ teaspoons adobo seasoning or garlic salt
Black pepper, to taste
1 (200g) can of tomato sauce
240ml water
1 small red pepper, sliced ½ cm thin strips
½ medium onion, sliced into ½cm thin strips
45g green pitted olives + 2 tablespoons of brine

1. Season the steak pieces with the adobo and black pepper. 2. Place the steak pieces in the baking pan, top them with the onions and peppers, then pour the tomato sauce and water over them. 3. Add the olives along with some of the brine (liquid from the jar). 4. Cook the food at 135°C for 8 hours on Slow Cook mode. 5. Once done, serve.

Per Serving: Calories 397; Fat 20.37g; Sodium 636mg; Carbs 19.83g; Fibre 1.3g; Sugar 1.16g; Protein 33.89g

Mini Beef Burger

Prep Time: 20 minutes | **Cook Time:** 20 minutes | **Serves:** 12

675g lean beef mince
80g yellow onion, chopped
2 teaspoon garlic, minced
2 tablespoons ketchup
2 tablespoons sweet pickle relish
1 tablespoon yellow mustard
1 tablespoon Cajun seasoning
½ teaspoon salt
¼ teaspoon ground black pepper, for seasoning
12 small dinner rolls, or hamburger buns
Slices of lettuce

1. In a large bowl, add onion, beef, garlic, pickle relish, ketchup, mustard, cajun seasoning, salt, and black pepper. Mix them until well combined. 2. Make the mixture into patties, about ¼ cup for each. Arrange the patties evenly on the cooking tray. 3. Air fry the fries at 205°C for 18 to 20 minutes. 4. When the cooking has done, make your own bam burgers as you like. 5. Serve and enjoy!

Per Serving: Calories 213; Fat 8.52g; Sodium 391mg; Carbs 15.59g; Fibre 1.4g; Sugar 2.1g; Protein 17.73g

Lemon Lamb Chops

Prep Time: 5 minutes | **Cook Time:** 15 minutes | **Serves:** 4

8 loin lamb chops
2 tablespoons mustard
½ teaspoon olive oil
1 teaspoon tarragon
1 tablespoon lemon juice
Salt and pepper

1. Mix the olive oil, tarragon, lemon juice, and mustard in a suitable bowl. 2. Rinse the lamb chops and drain. Pat them dry. 3. Brush the lamb chops with the mustard-herb mixture. 4. Arrange the lamb chops evenly in the cooking tray. 5. Air fry the lamb chops at 105°C for 15 minutes. 6. Flip them once halfway through cooking. 7. Carefully remove from the air fryer. 8. Serve and enjoy!

Per Serving: Calories 198; Fat 8.6g; Sodium 174mg; Carbs 1.16g; Fibre 0.5g; Sugar 0.17g; Protein 27.54g

Roasted Skirt Steaks

Prep Time: 10 minutes | **Cook Time:** 10 minutes | **Serves:** 2

2 (200g Skirt Steaks
30g finely chopped parsley
5g finely chopped mint
2 tablespoons fresh oregano (Washed & finely chopped)
3 finely chopped cloves of garlic
1 teaspoon red pepper flakes (Crushed)
1 tablespoon ground cumin
1 teaspoon cayenne pepper
2 teaspoons smoked paprika
1 teaspoon salt
¼ teaspoon pepper
180ml oil
3 tablespoons red wine vinegar

1. Mix up all the ingredients except for the steaks in the bowl. 2. Add ¼ cup of the mixture in a plastic baggie with the steak and place in the refrigerator overnight. 3. Allow it to sit for at least 30 minutes at room temperature, and then arrange the steaks on the cooking tray. 4. Roast the food at 200°C for 10 minutes. 5. Once done, serve and enjoy.

Per Serving: Calories 1043; Fat 96.89g; Sodium 1663mg; Carbs 8.39g; Fibre 3.3g; Sugar 1.13g; Protein 39.04g

Pork Chops

Prep Time: 5 minutes | **Cook Time:** 30 minutes | **Serves:** 3

455g boneless pork chops or 3 pieces, 1 cm thick
1 tablespoon olive oil
½ teaspoon salt
1 teaspoon paprika
1 teaspoon garlic powder
1 teaspoon onion powder
¼ teaspoon ground black pepper
½ teaspoon Italian seasoning

1. Mix up all the ingredients except for the oil and pork chops in a mixing bowl. 2. Coat the pork chops on both sides with the olive oil and then with the spice mixture. 3. Arrange the pork chops evenly in the baking pan. 4. Bake the pork chops at 165°C for 30 minutes. 5. When done, serve and enjoy.

Per Serving: Calories 243; Fat 9.79g; Sodium 497mg; Carbs 2.43g; Fibre 0.6g; Sugar 0.4g; Protein 34.34g

Rib-eye Steak

Prep Time: 15 minutes | **Cook Time:** 10 minutes | **Serves:** 6 8

1 (1.2kg to 1.5kg) tomahawk steak
Salt and freshly ground pepper
1 tablespoon butter if desired

1. Leave the steak on the countertop to room temperature. 2. Set the air fryer to Bake function, and adjust the temperature to 120°C and time to 50 minutes. Press Start/Stop to begin. 3. When the cooking time is up, let the air fryer stand for 5 to 15 minutes. 4. Grill the steak at 205°C for 2 minutes until the steak is just browned, flipping it once halfway through. 5. Carefully remove the dish from the air fryer. 6. Serve and enjoy!

Per Serving: Calories 515; Fat 27.55g; Sodium 792mg; Carbs 23.43g; Fibre 0.9g; Sugar 0.17g; Protein 43.26g

Mongolian Beef

Prep Time: 10 minutes | **Cook Time:** 10 minutes | **Serves:** 4

455g flank steak, sliced
30g cornflour
2 tablespoons olive oil
4 cloves minced garlic
1 tablespoon minced ginger
120ml low sodium soy sauce
120ml water
110g brown sugar
2 green onions, chopped

1. Coat the beef slices with the cornflour and then set aside for 5 minutes. 2. Spritz the beef slices with oil and then arrange them in the baking pan. 3. Air fry the beef slices at 205°C for 10 minutes. 4. Flip the meat slices every few minutes and spritz them with additional oil halfway through the cooking process. 5. Heat the olive oil and stir fry the ginger and garlic in the frying pan. 6. Add the meat slices and cook for 2 minutes. 7. In the saucepan, stir together the soy sauce, water, and brown sugar; bring them to boil and simmer for 6 to 7 minutes, stirring periodically, or until the sauce has thickened. 8. Carefully add the cooked beef mixture to the sauce and continue cooking for 1 to 2 minutes, tossing the beef in the sauce. 9. Sprinkle chopped green onions and sesame seeds (optional) over the top before serving.

Per Serving: Calories 383; Fat 12.71g; Sodium 1222mg; Carbs 39.35g; Fibre 1g; Sugar 28.28g; Protein 27.8g

Simple-Seasoned Beef

Prep Time: 10 minutes | **Cook Time:** 20 minutes | **Serves:** 6

½ teaspoon fresh rosemary
1 teaspoon dried thyme
¼ teaspoon black pepper
1 teaspoon salt
1.8kg top round roast beef
1 teaspoon olive oil

1. Combine the thyme, rosemary, salt, and pepper in a bowl. 2. Rub the beef on all sides with the olive oil and the thyme mixture. 3. Transfer the beef to the cooking tray. 4. Roast the beef at 180°C for 20 minutes. 5. When done, let the beef sit for 10 minutes before serving.

Per Serving: Calories 382; Fat 10.62g; Sodium 557mg; Carbs 0.12g; Fibre 0.1g; Sugar 0g; Protein 71.4g

Beef Kebabs

Prep Time: 10 minutes | **Cook Time:** 18 minutes | **Serves:** 4

2 teaspoons ground cumin
2 teaspoons ground coriander
¼ teaspoon ground cinnamon
⅛ teaspoon ground smoked paprika
2 teaspoons lime zest
½ teaspoon salt
½ teaspoon black pepper
1 tablespoon lemon juice
2 teaspoons olive oil
675g of Lean beef, cubed

1. Prepare all the ingredients and then mix them together in a large mixing bowl. 2. Thread the beef on the skewers. 3. Place the beef skewers in the cooking tray. 4. Air fry the skewers at 190°C for 18 minutes. 5. Flip the skewers when cooked halfway through. 6. Serve warm.

Per Serving: Calories 253; Fat 12.23g; Sodium 439mg; Carbs 1.37g; Fibre 0.4g; Sugar 0.18g; Protein 35.18g

Roasted Steak

Prep Time: 25 minutes | **Cook Time:** 20 minutes | **Serves:** 2

4 tablespoons butter, softened
2 cloves garlic, minced
2 teaspoons freshly chopped parsley
1 teaspoon freshly chopped chives
1 teaspoon freshly chopped thyme
1 teaspoon freshly chopped rosemary
1 (900g) bone-in rib-eye steak
Salt
Freshly ground black pepper

1. Mix the butter together with the chopped parsley, chopped chives, chopped thyme, chopped rosemary, and garlic in a bowl. 2. Place the butter mixture in the centre of a piece of plastic wrap and roll it into a log; twist the ends to keep tight, and then refrigerate the mixture for 20 minutes until it hardens. 3. Rub the steak with salt and pepper on both sides to season. 4. Arrange the steak on the cooking tray. 5. Roast the steak at 205°C for 20 minutes. 6. Flip the steak every 10 minutes to promote even browning until the steak has an internal temperature of 62°C and the steak is nicely browned. 7. Let the steak cool briefly before serving. 8. Garnish the steak with the butter mixture and enjoy.

Per Serving: Calories 805; Fat 70.92g; Sodium 392mg; Carbs 2.02g; Fibre 0.5g; Sugar 0.07g; Protein 41.5g

BBQ Pork Ribs

Prep Time: 10 minutes | **Cook Time:** 15 minutes | **Serves:** 6

85g honey, divided
180g BBQ sauce
2 tablespoons tomato ketchup
1 tablespoon Worcestershire sauce
1 tablespoon soy sauce
½ teaspoon garlic powder
Freshly ground white pepper to taste
800g pork ribs

1. Mix up the BBQ sauce, tomato ketchup, Worcestershire sauce, soy sauce, garlic powder, white pepper, and 3 tablespoons of honey in the bowl. 2. Add the pork ribs and then place the bowl in the refrigerator to marinate the ribs for 20 minutes. 3. Roast the pork ribs at 180°C for 13 minutes. 4. When cooked, remove the ribs from the Air Fryer and coat them with the remaining honey. 5. Serve hot.

Per Serving: Calories 251; Fat 8.03g; Sodium 389mg; Carbs 15.87g; Fibre 0.8g; Sugar 14.12g; Protein 28.4g

Pork Tenderloin with Peach Salsa

Prep Time: 15 minutes | **Cook Time:** 22 minutes | **Serves:** 4

115g fresh peaches, peeled and chopped
1 small sweet red pepper, chopped
1 jalapeno pepper, seeded and chopped
2 tablespoons red onion, finely chopped
2 tablespoons fresh coriander, minced
1 tablespoon lime juice
1 garlic clove, minced
⅛ teaspoon salt
⅛ teaspoon pepper
2 tablespoons olive oil
1 tablespoon brown sugar
1 tablespoon Caribbean jerk seasoning
1 teaspoon dried thyme
1 teaspoon dried rosemary, crushed
½ teaspoon seasoned salt
455g pork tenderloin

1. Add chopped peaches, red pepper, jalapeno pepper, red onion, minced coriander, lime juice, garlic, salt, and pepper in a small bowl and combine well. 2. Add brown sugar, thyme, rosemary, seasoned salt, oil, and jerk seasoning in a separate bowl and mix well. 3. Rub the pork tenderloin with the mixture. 4. Air fry the pork tenderloin at 170°C for 22 minutes, flipping them halfway through. 5. When the pork has been done, the internal meat thermometer should read 63°C. 6. Cool the dish for about 5 minutes after cooking. 7. Cut into your desired-sized slices. 8. Serve and enjoy!

Per Serving: Calories 285; Fat 10.88g; Sodium 592mg; Carbs 15.66g; Fibre 1.6g; Sugar 12.63g; Protein 30.39g

Butter Sirloin Steaks

Prep Time: 10 minutes | **Cook Time:** 45 minutes | **Serves:** 2

2 top sirloin steaks
3 tablespoons butter, melted
3 tablespoons olive oil
Salt and pepper to taste

1. Season the sirloin steaks with olive oil, salt, and pepper; arrange the seasoned steaks on the cooking tray. 2. Roast the steaks at 175°C for 45 minutes. 3. When done, serve the steaks with melted butter.

Per Serving: Calories 1463; Fat 103.68g; Sodium 454mg; Carbs 2.14g; Fibre 0.3g; Sugar 1.16g; Protein 123.47g

Flavourful Leg of Lamb

Prep Time: 10 minutes | **Cook Time:** 6 hours 30 minutes | **Serves:** 8

12 cloves of garlic, peeled
3.1kg of leg of lamb
Salt and pepper
3 teaspoons paprika powder
3 teaspoons garlic powder
2 tablespoons olive oil
2 large onions, quartered
10 sprigs of thyme
3 sprigs rosemary
3 teaspoons dried oregano
3 dried bay leaves
120ml lemon juice
360ml white wine
480ml chicken stock

1. Slit the lamb with a small knife on the top. 2. Cut about half the garlic cloves into slivers and stuff them into the slits. 3. Sprinkle salt, garlic powder, pepper, and paprika all over the lamb. Drizzle them with olive oil and rub for a marinade. 4. Add the lamb to the baking pan. 5. Roast the fries at 205°C for 30 minutes until a nice brown crust has shown. 6. Carefully remove the pan from the air fryer. Adjust the temperature to 175°C and time to 6 hours. 7. Turn the lamb upside down. Add all the remaining ingredients to the pan around the lamb. Pour in hot water until it comes up about a quarter to a third of the way up the height of the lamb. 8. Cover the lamb with parchment paper, then 2 layers of foil. 9. Let it roast in the air fryer for 3 hours and 30 minutes. 10. Add water to prevent it from drying out. Discover and turn the lamb. 11. Cover and roast for 2 hours and 30 minutes. 12. When the cooking time is up, remove the cover and roast for 20 to 30 minutes until brown. 13. Carefully remove from the air fryer. Transfer to a serving plate and use a foil to cover loosely. Let it rest for 30 to 40 minutes. 14. Reserve the liquid in a clear jug and skim the oil. Add lemon juice, salt, and pepper to season. 15. Serve and enjoy!

Per Serving: Calories 604; Fat 24.73g; Sodium 518mg; Carbs 9.17g; Fibre 1.6g; Sugar 3.3g; Protein 82.07g

Vegetables & Bacon Burgers

Prep Time: 10 minutes | **Cook Time:** 40 minutes | **Serves:** 4

4 slices of thick-cut bacon
200g shiitake or cremini mushrooms, thinly sliced
220g onions, thinly sliced
½ teaspoon garlic, minced
Salt, for seasoning
Ground black pepper for seasoning
4 (150g) hamburger patties
4 slices of Swiss cheese
4 onion buns, halved and toasted
Mayonnaise, for serving (optional)
Mustard, for serving (optional)

1. Place the bacon slices on the baking pan. 2. Line a plate with a paper towel. 3. When the bacon slices are cooked, place the bacon slices onto the paper towel-lined plate, removing half of the fat from the baking pan and reserving half of the fat on the pan. 4. Add the mushrooms to the baking pan. 5. Air fry the mushrooms at 205°C for 6 minutes. 6. Transfer the cooked mushrooms to a dish. 7. Place the hamburger patties on the cooking tray. 8. Air fry the patties at 205°C for 10 minutes. 9. While cooking the hamburger patties, mix up the mushrooms, onions, garlic, salt, and black pepper in a bowl. 10. When the hamburger patties are cooked, place a mound of mushrooms, onions, and Swiss cheese on each hamburger patty, and then air fry them at 205°C for 2 minutes. 11. Place the hamburger patties between the buns, top each patty with the bacon, and dress in the mayonnaise and mustard (optional). 12. Enjoy.

Per Serving: Calories 485; Fat 30.32g; Sodium 462mg; Carbs 33.53g; Fibre 4.7g; Sugar 9.83g; Protein 22.21g

Short Beef Ribs

Prep Time: 10 minutes | **Cook Time:** 10 minutes | **Serves:** 6

2.7kg of beef short ribs
1 pinch salt
1 teaspoon liquid crab boil
350g ketchup
300ml of light beer
1 tablespoon molasses
1 pinch freshly ground black pepper
1 tablespoon Creole or whole-grain mustard
1 tablespoon garlic, chopped
80g onions, chopped
55g firmly packed light brown sugar
1 dash of hot pepper sauce
1 dash Worcestershire sauce
1 pinch of ground cayenne pepper
1 tablespoon fresh ginger, peeled and grated

1. Rub the ribs with salt and black pepper. Place in a 4.5 L Dutch oven. 2. Process together the ketchup, mustard, beef, onions, garlic, hot pepper sauce, Worcester sauce, ground cayenne pepper, 1 teaspoon black pepper, molasses, 1 teaspoon salt, light beer, ginger, and crab boil in a food processor. Blend them for 15 seconds until smooth. 3. Arrange the ribs onto the baking pan and pour the sauce mixture over the ribs. Cover the pan. 4. Cook the ribs at 205°C for 8 minutes on Slow Cook mode. 5. When the cooking time is up, carefully remove it from the air fryer. 6. Serve the ribs with sauce. Enjoy!

Per Serving: Calories 925; Fat 44.38g; Sodium 1136mg; Carbs 39.06g; Fibre 0.7g; Sugar 29.69g; Protein 95.57g

Simple Lamb Chops

Prep Time: 15 minutes | **Cook Time:** 35 minutes | **Serves:** 4

1 L buttermilk
60ml hot sauce
3 tablespoons garlic, minced
2 teaspoons celery salt
2⅓ teaspoons salt, divided
2⅓ teaspoons black pepper, divided
4 lamb chops,
4 eggs
120ml milk
500g flour

1. In a mixing bowl, add hot sauce, buttermilk, garlic, celery salt, 2 teaspoons of salt, and 1 teaspoon of black pepper, and stir them well. 2. Evenly coat the lamb chops with the buttermilk mixture and then leave the lamb chops in the mixture; cover the bowl and place in the refrigerator to marinate the lamb chops overnight. 3. Remove the marinade and let the lamb chops sit at room temperature for about 1 hour. 4. Stir the eggs with the milk well in a bowl. 5. Combine the flour, ⅓ teaspoon of salt, and 1⅓ teaspoon of black pepper in another bowl. 6. Dip the lamb chops into the flour mixture and shake off any excess, then dip them into the egg mixture and lastly, dip them into the flour mixture again. 7. Grease the baking pan with the cooking spray and then place the lamb chops on it. 8. Air fry the lamb chops at 205°C for 35 minutes. 9. When done, the lamp chops should have an internal temperature of 70°C.

Per Serving: Calories 994; Fat 30.52g; Sodium 2598mg; Carbs 113.81g; Fibre 4g; Sugar 14.79g; Protein 61.56g

Homemade Pork Tenderloin

Prep Time: 10 minutes | **Cook Time:** 15 minutes | **Serves:** 4

3 tablespoons Dijon mustard
3 tablespoons honey
1 teaspoon dried rosemary
1 tablespoon olive oil
455g pork tenderloin, rinsed and drained
Salt and black pepper to taste

1. In the bowl, mix up the honey, Dijon mustard, and rosemary. 2. Rub the pork tenderloin with salt and pepper on all sides. 3. In the frying pan over high heat, heat the olive oil; add the pork tenderloin and cook for 3 minutes on each side, until golden brown. 4. Turn off the heat, evenly coat the pork tenderloin with the honey mixture and then transfer the pork tenderloin to the baking pan. 5. Bake the food at 215°C for 15 minutes. 6. When done, the pork tenderloin should have an inner temperature of 62°C. 7. Allow the pork tenderloin to sit for 3 minutes before slicing and serving.

Per Serving: Calories 249; Fat 7.77g; Sodium 194mg; Carbs 14.06g; Fibre 0.7g; Sugar 13.04g; Protein 30.23g

Chapter 7 Desserts Recipes

Cinnamon Bread Pudding

Prep Time: 5 minutes | **Cook Time:** 20 minutes | **Serves:** 2

125g Cubed cinnamon-raisin bread
1 large egg
160ml low fat milk
3 tablespoons Brown sugar
1 tablespoon melted butter
½ teaspoon Ground cinnamon
¼ teaspoon Ground nutmeg
Dash salt
50g Raisins

1. Grease the muffin cups and apportion the bread cubes between them. 2. Mix up the brown sugar, milk, butter, egg, salt, nutmeg, and cinnamon in a bowl; stir in the raisins, and then pour the mixture over the bread cubes. 3. Let the food stand for 15 minutes before baking. 4. Bake the food at 175°C for 15 minutes. 5. When done, transfer the food to the serving plate.

Per Serving: Calories 195; Fat 11.51g; Sodium 218mg; Carbs 25.31g; Fibre 1.1g; Sugar 16.91g; Protein 5.29g

Blueberry Crumble

Prep Time: 10 minutes | **Cook Time:** 20 minutes | **Serves:** 4

80g fresh apricots, de-stoned and cubed
150g fresh blueberries
100g sugar
1 tablespoon lemon juice
125g flour
Salt, to taste
1 tablespoon butter

1. Mix the apricot with the lemon juice, blueberries, and two tablespoons of sugar in a bowl. 2. Evenly spread the apricot mixture on the greased baking pan. 3. In another bowl, mix up the flour, the remaining sugar, one tablespoon of cold water, and the butter until the mixture is crumbly. 4. Top the apricot mixture with the flour mixture. 5. Bake the mixture at 200°C for 20 minutes. 6. When done, serve and enjoy.

Per Serving: Calories 284; Fat 3.49g; Sodium 66mg; Carbs 60.88g; Fibre 3.1g; Sugar 34.19g; Protein 4.24g

Homemade Smores

Prep Time: 5 minutes | **Cook Time:** 10 minutes | **Serves:** 4

8 digestive biscuits
4 large marshmallows
1 milk chocolate bar

1. Place the four biscuits in the cooking tray. 2. Cut a small slice of the marshmallows and stick it to the biscuits. 3. Air fry the crackers at 190°C for 10 minutes. 4. After 8 minutes of cooking, evenly apportion the chocolate bar between the marshmallows and top them with another digestive biscuit. 5. Resume baking them for 2 minutes. 6. When done, serve and enjoy.

Per Serving: Calories 83; Fat 2.85g; Sodium 39mg; Carbs 14.32g; Fibre 0.4g; Sugar 9.79g; Protein 1.05g

Cinnamon Apricot

Prep Time: 10 minutes | **Cook Time:** 30 minutes | **Serves:** 6

For the filling:

990g apricots, pitted and sliced
½ teaspoon ground ginger
1 tablespoon cornflour
160g maple syrup
½ teaspoon cinnamon
½ teaspoon lemon zest

For the topping:

90g plain flour
80g old-fashioned oats
3 tablespoons brown sugar
6 tablespoons butter, cubed
1 teaspoon cinnamon
¼ teaspoon salt

1. Grease the baking pan with the cooking spray. 2. Add all the filling ingredients to the bowl and mix them well. 3. Mix up all the topping ingredients and then sprinkle them over the filling mixture. 4. Transfer the mixture to the baking pan. 5. Bake the mixture at 175°C for 30 minutes. 6. Serve and enjoy after cooking.

Per Serving: Calories 602; Fat 13.47g; Sodium 206mg; Carbs 127.21g; Fibre 12.7g; Sugar 89.56g; Protein 8.91g

Vanilla Pecan Brownies

Prep Time: 10 minutes | **Cook Time:** 35 minutes | **Serves:** 12

2 eggs, lightly beaten
125g plain flour
430g brown sugar
115g butter softened
80g pecan pieces
1 teaspoon vanilla
1 teaspoon baking powder

1. Grease the baking pan with the cooking spray. 2. Beat the eggs with butter and brown sugar in a bowl; add the flour, vanilla, baking powder, and pecans, then mix them until well combined. 3. Pour the mixture into the baking pan. 4. Bake the food at 175°C for 35 minutes. 5. When done, let the brownies cool for a while before serving.

Serving Suggestion: Slice and serve.
Variation Tip: You can add chopped walnuts instead of pecans.

Per Serving: Calories 234; Fat 13.62g; Sodium 114mg; Carbs 25.97g; Fibre 0.9g; Sugar 16.88g; Protein 2.98g

Butter Peanut Cookies

Prep Time: 10 minutes | **Cook Time:** 5 minutes | **Serves:** 10

1 egg
255g peanut butter
200g sugar

1. Line the baking pan with parchment paper. 2. Mix up all the ingredients in the bowl, and then form the mixture into cookies. 3. Place the cookies on the prepared baking pan. 4. Air fry the cookies at 175°C for 5 minutes. 5. When done, serve and enjoy.

Per Serving: Calories 126; Fat 5.58g; Sodium 396mg; Carbs 16.42g; Fibre 0.5g; Sugar 14.76g; Protein 2.71g

Apple Fritters

Prep Time: 5 minutes | **Cook Time:** 10 minutes | **Serves:** 4

65g self-rising flour
50g coconut flour
240g sour cream
100g granulated sugar
1 teaspoon ground cinnamon
½ teaspoon ground cardamom
1 large apple, peeled, cored, and grated

1. Grease the baking pan with the oil or cooking spray. 2. Mix up all the ingredients in a large bowl. 3. Form the mixture into equal-sized fritters and place them on the baking pan. 4. Air fry the fritters at 165°C for 10 minutes. 5. Turn the fritters halfway through. 6. When the time is up, serve and enjoy.

Per Serving: Calories 219; Fat 6.43g; Sodium 267mg; Carbs 37.66g; Fibre 2.5g; Sugar 18.98g; Protein 3.97g

Pumpkin Muffins

Prep Time: 10 minutes | **Cook Time:** 20 minutes | **Serves:** 6

2 eggs
1 tablespoon pumpkin spice
1 teaspoon baking powder
3 tablespoons Swerve
1 tablespoon coconut flour
150g almond flour
¼ teaspoon liquid stevia
8 tablespoons butter, melted

1. Line the baking pan with cupcake liners. 2. Mix the eggs, sweetener, and butter in a bowl until well combined, then add the remaining ingredients and mix them well. 3. Bake the food at 150°C for 15 to 20 minutes. 4. When done, serve and enjoy.

Per Serving: Calories 186; Fat 18.9g; Sodium 160mg; Carbs 1.56g; Fibre 0.2g; Sugar 0.39g; Protein 3.29g

Cinnamon Pear Halves

Prep Time: 10 minutes | **Cook Time:** 25 minutes | **Serves:** 4

4 pears, cut in half and cored
1 teaspoon vanilla
¼ teaspoon cinnamon
160g maple syrup

1. Mix up the maple syrup and vanilla in the bowl. 2. Arrange the pear halves in the baking pan, sprinkle them with the cinnamon and drizzle the vanilla mixture over them. 3. Bake the pears at 190°C for 25 minutes. 4. When done, transfer the pears to the serving plate.

Per Serving: Calories 162; Fat 0.13g; Sodium 9mg; Carbs 41.24g; Fibre 1.3g; Sugar 35.49g; Protein 0.18g

Tasty Chocolate Donuts

Prep Time: 10 minutes | **Cook Time:** 10 minutes | **Serves:** 8

125g plain flour
1 teaspoon vanilla
2 tablespoons butter, melted
1 egg, lightly beaten
120ml buttermilk
100g granulated sugar
½ teaspoon baking soda
20g unsweetened cocoa powder
⅛ teaspoon salt

1. Spray a donut pan with cooking spray. 2. Combine the flour, baking soda, cocoa powder, and salt in a mixing bowl. 3. Whisk the egg, vanilla, butter, sugar, and buttermilk in another bowl until well combined. 4. Pour the egg mixture into the flour mixture and mix until just combined. 5. Spoon the batter into the prepared donut pan. 6. Bake the food at 175°C for 10 minutes. 7. When done, serve and enjoy.

Per Serving: Calories 135; Fat 4.56g; Sodium 210mg; Carbs 20.75g; Fibre 1.2g; Sugar 7.2g; Protein 3.58g

Hazelnut Chocolate Brownies

Prep Time: 10 minutes | **Cook Time:** 20 minutes | **Serves:** 8

1 egg
50g flour
55g butter
50g chocolate, chopped
25g hazelnuts, chopped
1 teaspoon vanilla
65g caster sugar

1. Grease the baking pan with oil or cooking spray. 2. In the saucepan over low heat, melt the chocolate. 3. Turn off the heat, stir the chocolate well and set it aside to cool. 4. Whisk the egg, vanilla, and sugar in a bowl; when the mixture is creamy, add melted chocolate mixture and flour and mix them until well combined. 5. Pour the mixture into the baking pan. 6. Air fry the mixture at 180°C for 18 to 20 minutes. 7. When done, serve and enjoy.

Per Serving: Calories 171; Fat 9.27g; Sodium 64mg; Carbs 19.65g; Fibre 0.7g; Sugar 12.51g; Protein 2.59g

Conclusion

An air fryer is very similar in function to a mini convection oven. It works by circulating hot air around the food, using less oil than traditional frying methods. This results in crispy food on the outside and cooked evenly throughout - perfect for French fries, chicken wings, and more! Besides being a healthier alternative to deep frying, air frying can also reduce cooking time. When using an air fryer, it's important to remember a few key things. First, don't overcrowd the basket - this will cause uneven cooking. Second, be sure to shake or flip food halfway through cooking to ensure even browning. And lastly, keep an eye on your food as it cooks, as air fryers can cook quickly and sometimes unexpectedly! With these tips in mind, you're well on the way to becoming an air fryer pro. Air fryers are a great and healthy way to cook food without all the added oil. They help you avoid adding unhealthy fats and provide a quick and easy cooking option for busy families. If you're trying to find a healthy and convenient way to cook your food, or if you just want an easier way to get dinner on the table, an air fryer is definitely worth considering.

Appendix 1 Measurement Conversion Chart

VOLUME EQUIVALENTS (LIQUID)

US STANDARD	US STANDARD (OUNCES)	METRIC (APPROXIMATE)
2 tablespoons	1 fl.oz	30 mL
¼ cup	2 fl.oz	60 mL
½ cup	4 fl.oz	120 mL
1 cup	8 fl.oz	240 mL
1½ cup	12 fl.oz	355 mL
2 cups or 1 pint	16 fl.oz	475 mL
4 cups or 1 quart	32 fl.oz	1 L
1 gallon	128 fl.oz	4 L

VOLUME EQUIVALENTS (DRY)

US STANDARD	METRIC (APPROXIMATE)
⅛ teaspoon	0.5 mL
¼ teaspoon	1 mL
½ teaspoon	2 mL
¾ teaspoon	4 mL
1 teaspoon	5 mL
1 tablespoon	15 mL
¼ cup	59 mL
½ cup	118 mL
¾ cup	177 mL
1 cup	235 mL
2 cups	475 mL
3 cups	700 mL
4 cups	1 L

TEMPERATURES EQUIVALENTS

FAHRENHEIT (F)	CELSIUS (C) (APPROXIMATE)
225℉	107℃
250℉	120℃
275℉	135℃
300℉	150℃
325℉	160℃
350℉	180℃
375℉	190℃
400℉	205℃
425℉	220℃
450℉	235℃
475℉	245℃
500℉	260℃

WEIGHT EQUIVALENTS

US STANDARD	METRIC (APPROXINATE)
1 ounce	28 g
2 ounces	57 g
5 ounces	142 g
10 ounces	284 g
15 ounces	425g
16 ounces (1 pound)	455 g
1.5pounds	680 g
2pounds	907g

Appendix 2 Recipes Index

A

Apple Fritters   71
Avocado Fries   31

B

Baked Cinnamon Rolls   26
Baked Turkey Breast   50
BBQ Pork Ribs   65
Beef and Broccoli Florets   60
Beef Kebabs   64
Blueberry Crumble   69
Braised Steak   61
Breaded Cod Fillets   41
Breaded Courgette Sticks   28
Butter Banana Bread   24
Butter Peanut Cookies   70
Butter Sirloin Steaks   65
Buttermilk Biscuits   23

C

Cauliflower Fritters   24
Cauliflower Fritters with Parmesan   40
Cauliflower Tacos   38
Cheese Broccoli Gratin   36
Cheese Fillets   45
Cheese Onion Stuffed Peppers   25
Cheese Sausage Frittata   22
Cheese Spinach Rolls   29
Cheese Stuffed Mushrooms   40
Chicken Pot Pie   50
Chicken Thighs with Sesame Seeds   54
Chicken Wings with Teriyaki Sauce   53
Chickpeas Falafels with Tahini Sauce   39
Chili Tilapia   41
Cinnamon Apricot   70
Cinnamon Bread Pudding   69
Cinnamon Pear Halves   71
Cod Fillets   45
Crab Meat Prawn Roll   48
Cream Chicken Parmigiana   52
Crisp Flounder Fillets   43
Crispy Cheese Sticks   29
Crispy Potato Chips   29

Crispy Pumpkin Seeds   28
Crispy Sweet Potato Chips   32
Crumbled Sausage Pizza   23
Crunchy Chicken Strips   52
Crusted Chicken Tenders   30
Crusted Chicken Thighs   51
Curry Chicken Wings   55

D

Dijon Feta Shakshuka   26

E

Easy Egg Rolls   23
Easy French Fries   28
Egg Potato Burrito   27
Egg Toast Cups   24
Exotic Chicken Meatballs   32

F

Fish Fingers   47
Fish Pineapple Mix   46
Flavourful Leg of Lamb   66
Flavourful Parmesan Aubergine   35
Flavourful Tilapia Fillets   42
Flounder Fillets   49
Fried Catfish Fillets   43
Fried Potato Pieces   22
Fried Ravioli   32

G

Garlicky Salmon   44
Golden Onion Rings   37
Green Beans and Mushrooms   35
Grilled Corn   30
Grilled Lobster Tail   44

H

Ham Omelet with Vegetable   21
Hazelnut Chocolate Brownies   72
Herb Chicken Thighs   56
Herbed Cauliflower Florets   34
Herbed Turkey Roast   56
Homemade Popcorn Chicken   57
Homemade Pork Tenderloin   68

Homemade Smores 69
Honey-Glazed Pork Chops 61
Hot Fried Chicken 55

J

Jumbo Lump Crab Cakes 44

L

Lemon Lamb Chops 62
Lemon-Flavored Salmon 42

M

Mac & Cheese Balls 33
Mackerel Fillets 46
Marinated Turkey Thighs 58
Mini Beef Burger 62
Mini Tofu Bites 39
Mongolian Beef 63

O

Onion & Sweet Potato 35

P

Palatable Brussels Sprouts 34
Panko Chicken Wings 59
Panko-Crusted Prawn 41
Parmesan Brussels Sprout 37
Peanut Butter Chicken Thighs 52
Polenta Squid 47
Pork Chops 63
Pork Tenderloin with Peach Salsa 65
Potato Pancakes 25
Prawn Stuffed Peppers 49
Pumpkin Muffins 71

R

Red Potatoes & Peppers 22
Red Snapper with Lemon Slices 43
Rib-eye Steak 63
Roasted Skirt Steaks 62
Roasted Steak 64
Rosemary Lamb Roast 61
Rosemary Salmon 42
Rustic Whole Chicken 51

S

Salmon in Honey-Miso Sauce 21

Savory Chicken Breasts 53
Savory Chickpeas 30
Seasoned Prawn 47
Short Beef Ribs 67
Simple Cheese Balls 38
Simple Lamb Chops 67
Simple-Seasoned Beef 64
Spiced Chicken in Egg Mixture 54
Spiced Pumpkin Pieces 36
Spiced Turkey Breast 59
Spicy Okra Fries 34
Spinach Pie with Cheese 25
Steak with Chimichurri Sauce 60
Strawberry Almonds Porridge 21

T

Tangy Cauliflower 37
Tasty Chocolate Donuts 72
Tasty Crackers 31
Tasty Salmon Fillets 46
Tilapia Tacos with Sauce 48
Tofu Cubes 36
Tuna Cakes 45
Turkey Breast and Bacon 58

V

Vanilla Pecan Brownies 70
Vegetables & Bacon Burgers 66
Veggies & Chicken Breasts 53
Veggies Chicken Pie 57

W

Walnut Courgette Bread 27
Whole Cooked Chicken 51
Wrapped Avocado 31

Printed in Great Britain
by Amazon